DOES LIFE BEGIN AT FORTYSOMETHING?

Age Forty: John Glenn is the first American astronaut to orbit the earth.

Forty-one: Christopher Columbus lands in the New World.

Forty-two: Satchell Paige joins the major leagues—as a rookie.

Forty-three: Clarence Birdseye puts the first frozen food on the market.

Forty-four: Saddam Hussein becomes president of Iraq.

Forty-five: Tina Turner wins a Grammy for "What's Love Got to Do with It?"

You'll learn all this and more
in the book that answers
thousands of age-old questions!

THE BOOK OF AGES

J. F. Bierlein

BALLANTINE BOOKS • NEW YORK

Copyright © 1992 by J.F. Bierlein

All rights reserved under International and Pan-American Copyright Conventions. Published in the United States of America by Ballantine Books, a division of Random House, Inc., New York, and simultaneously in Canada by Random House of Canada Limited, Toronto.

Library of Congress Catalog Card Number: 91-93142

ISBN 0-345-37560-2

Manufactured in the United States of America

First Edition: April 1992

This book is dedicated to
RENEE,
whose presence in my life makes
me look forward to sharing new ages.

acknowledgments

I would like to thank all of the people who assisted me, encouraged me, and made helpful suggestions. I begin by thanking my parents, John and Veronica Bierlein. My father was a faithful editor, adviser, envelope addresser, and made some of the finest coffee available. My mother was a research assistant of the highest order and was a great source of suggestions about new entries. I also owe immense gratitude to Renee Pringle-Schoenknecht, whose editing, encouragement, love, and patience were essential to the completion of this book. Renee deserves a special thanks for finding me a computer printer at the eleventh hour. Robert Hirschfeld deserves my appreciation; without his encouragement and long conversations about the concept and execution of this book, there would be no *Book of Ages*. Each of these "nearest and dearest ones" leaves his or her mark in this book.

My thanks also to my friend and editor, Iris Bass, who was a delight to work with.

Many friends took an interest in this project and provided encouragement, prayers, and suggestions: Donna Kusky, Darlene Underhill, Dr. Steven Hirschfeld, Father Ken Bieber, Bryan Dugan, Monica Bischof, Lynn Hibbard, and the wonderful staff of the Hoyt Library, Saginaw, Michigan.

My sincere thanks to the many wonderful people who were there for me!

introduction

Why a *Book of Ages*? Age is important and age does not matter. Both are true.

Age defines our life-style: what we listen to, watch, wear, and eat are dictated by our popular culture's definitions of age. A major influence upon our economy is our youthfulness or our attempt to postpone and disguise our aging. Our true age, our maturity, and our experience color our lives.

Age must be important: it is the only thing that many otherwise honest people try hard to conceal or even lie about. I recently attended the birthday party of a "sixty-something" friend who both looks and acts considerably younger than his chronological years. He is reticent about discussing his actual age, and an entire roomful of people, some older and some younger, thoroughly entertained themselves for the better part of an evening by attempting to guess his birth year.

My own generation, the "baby boomers," are approaching middle age. Within only a few years, the vanguard of the generation will turn fifty. This is the same group that gave us the "youth" culture of the sixties and seventies, as well as the "yuppie" culture of the eighties. The midlife crises of this group have made excellent grist for the television and cinema mills.

Age defines public policy. The increased lifespan of our population and the costs of providing social security and health care are among the most important, and controversial, public questions. Likewise, the education and well-being of our children are at the center of public interest.

Age is important in understanding why people do what they do, and how they do it. Knowing the age composers, writers, actors, or painters were when they produced a given work may provide a valuable insight into the work itself. We who listen to, read, watch, or see the results benefit by knowing how much of life's experiences they brought to their creation. I have to wonder how many masterpieces remained unfinished until both the creator and the work reached a particular level of maturity.

Then again, age does *not* matter. Age, as the many entries in this book demonstrate, is not a barrier to achievement. It is more an excuse than a reason for timidity in the face of challenge. The creative are always creative, whatever their age; the expression of their creativity may change, but they continue to create.

This book is the product of many conversations I have had with friends over the years. These conversations typically began with "Here I am forty (or thirty or fifty) and what have I accomplished with my life?" I used to like to "season" these conversations with a few encouraging examples of people of their age who either had accomplished nothing—at least yet—or failed, or faced some grave hardship or obstacle on the way to great achievement. Looking at our own failures in comparison with those faced by others, we begin to see failure as the seed of achievement. Looking at the obstacles that others have had to overcome, ours seem very small.

The message of *The Book of Ages* is a message of hope. It is never too late to be great. There really is no such thing as permanent failure or a dead end in life. If we live in a state of permanent failure or seem to find ourselves at a dead end, it is only because we choose to limit our thinking. Some of the most inspiring and entertaining entries in this book are those that begin with tragedy, poverty, or disadvantage and end in greatness.

This book is, I hope, an entertaining source of trivia,

an argument settler, and a pleasant way to pass time. I also hope, however, that you don't miss the message while you have fun.

Another reason I wrote this book is that I see no greater area of factual error than ages. I encounter an incorrect age for a person at least once a week in newspapers, magazines, or books. Such mistakes really aren't necessary. There may be some errors in this book, but on the whole, I meticulously calculated the ages of people in the entries from the month of their birth, wherever possible, rather than merely subtracting one year from another. Generally, I used two sources to confirm the birth date of a subject. In the cases of some entertainers, I had to refer to more than six, or even a dozen, sources as several different birth dates were given. I have to wonder whether the entertainers themselves gave the wrong dates.

While working on this book, I tried several times to organize the entries alphabetically, by date, or by subject. Each attempt left me feeling that the book was a lot less entertaining. After putting the manuscript aside for a few days, I found that I liked a relatively random arrangement of the entries within a given age. For me, it reflected the variety and sometime randomness of our world, what the Book of Common Prayer calls "the changes and chances of this mortal life."

Although authoritative, my book makes no claim to be an exhaustive treatment of the subject. I continue to collect entries for my own pleasure. This may result in a second *Book of Ages*, and it may not. But, in gathering such entries, I enjoy a sense of the wonder of life and the greatness of its possibilities.

In compiling the entries, I tried to provide a fair sample of varying nationalities, races, and both genders. However, I feel that women are underrepresented. This is due largely to the preponderance of males in historical sources, and I attempted to remedy this as much as I could by providing outstanding examples of women, particularly in the arts. In gathering more entries for the future, I have been sensitive to this imbalance. Likewise, I have tried to achieve a reasonable racial balance.*

There is a great deal of "eurocentricism" inherent in relying on historical sources, which I have tried to balance as reasonably well as possible. Anyway, I am confident that I have demonstrated the possibilities of creative human endeavor at many chronological ages and within many cultures.

I hope that this book entertains, inspires, and informs you. But most important, I hope that this book will help you to wonder at life's possibilities even as you are entertained. And I hope that it gives you hope.

J. F. Bierlein

---

*One problem I encountered is the inconsistent use of "African-American" or "black" or "person of color." Our society has yet to determine the proper term, and authoritative historical sources use all three.

age one

"A baby is God's opinion that the world should go on."

—Carl Sandburg

BABY SANDY
makes her film debut as an infant in the films *East Side of Heaven*, *Unexpected Father*, and *Little Accident*, 1939.

BABY LEROY
appears in *A Bedtime Story*, *Torch Singer*, *Tillie and Gus*, and *Alice in Wonderland*, 1933.

JACKIE COOGAN
makes his film debut at age eighteen months in *Skinner's Baby*, 1917.

HUMPHREY BOGART
is an infant celebrity, 1900. His mother was the celebrated illustrator Maude Humphrey Bogart, and her painting of her infant son became the best-known baby picture of the day after it was adopted by a baby food company for its advertisements.

LOUIS XIV,
the future "sun king" of France, is born with two teeth, 1639 (*Guinness Book of World Records*).

age two

BABY LEROY
appears in the films *The Old-Fashioned Way*, *It's a Gift*, and *Miss Fane's Baby Is Stolen*, 1934. His contract had to be signed by his grandfather, as his mother was underage.

AISIN GORO PU YI
becomes the last Manchu emperor of China, 1908. His story is the basis of the 1987 Bernardo Bertolucci film, *The Last Emperor*.

age three

"SPANKY" MCFARLAND
makes his film debut in the *Our Gang* series of comedies,
syndicated on television as "The Little Rascals," 1932.

JOHN STUART MILL,
future British philosopher, learns classical Greek, 1809.

LEWIS MELVILLE "GINO" HALL
paints *Trees and Monkeys*, 1965. It would later be sub-
mitted to the Royal Academy of Art, London, and was
exhibited in 1967, making him, according to the *Guinness Book of World Records*, the youngest artist ever to
be exhibited.

age four

*"The greatest poem ever known
is one all poets have outgrown
The poetry, innate, untold
of being only four years old."*
                    —Christopher Morley

SHIRLEY TEMPLE
appears in her first film, *The Red-Haired Alibi*, 1932.

BABY LEROY
appears in *It's a Great Life*, and retires from motion pictures, 1936.

DARLA HOOD
debuts on *Our Gang* comedies, 1935. You may recall her as the romantic interest of Carl "Alfalfa" Switzer.

BABY SANDY
retires from motion pictures, 1942.

JACKIE COOGAN
appears with Charlie Chaplin in *A Day's Pleasure*, 1919.

DOROTHY STRAIGHT
according to *the Guinness Book of World Records*, is the youngest person ever to become a published author. In 1962, at age four, she wrote *How the World Began*, which was published in 1964.

age five

"Children are grateful to Santa Claus for filling their stockings with toys; why aren't their parents grateful to God for filling theirs with legs?"
—G. K. Chesterton

SHIRLEY TEMPLE
makes two films, *To the Last Man* and *Out All Night*, 1933. She received a special honorary Academy Award before her sixth birthday.

NATALIE WOOD
(born Natasha Gurdin) makes her film debut in *Happy Land*, 1942.

JACKIE COOGAN
appears with Charlie Chaplin in the silent classic *The Kid*, 1920.

MARSHAL DUKE OF CAXIAS
is listed in the *Guinness Book of World Records* as the youngest known soldier. He enlisted with an infantry unit of the Brazilian army, 1808.

age six

"My mother loved children—she would have given anything if I had been one."

—Groucho Marx

BABY PEGGY
appears in *Hollywood* and *The Darling of New York*, 1923. Baby Peggy was the "Shirley Temple" of the silent film era and Shirley Temple appeared in many sound versions of her films.

SHIRLEY TEMPLE
appears in nine films, 1934, including *Carolina*, *Mandalay*, *Stand Up and Cheer*, *Now I'll Tell*, *Change of Heart*, *Little Miss Marker*, *Baby Take a Bow*, and *Bright Eyes*.

age seven

MARVIN HAMLISCH
is the youngest person ever accepted to the Juilliard
School of Music, 1952.

BABY PEGGY
makes five movies, 1924, including *Captain January*, the
sound version of which was made by Shirley Temple in
1937.

SHIRLEY TEMPLE
makes *Curly Top*, *The Littlest Rebel*, and *The Little Colonel*, 1935.

YEHUDI MENUHIN
appears as a solo violinist with the San Francisco Symphony, 1923.

age eight

JACKIE COOPER
makes his film debut, 1929.

BABY PEGGY
makes two films, *The Speed Demon* and *Fighting Courage*, 1925.

SHIRLEY TEMPLE
appears in the sound version of *Captain January*, as well as *Poor Little Rich Girl*, *Dimples*, and *Stowaway*, 1936.

WOLFGANG AMADEUS MOZART
composes the first of a total of forty-one symphonies written during his lifetime, 1764.

LUIS ANTONIO DE BORBON
is the youngest person ever elected a cardinal of the Roman Catholic Church, 1735 (*Guinness Book of World Records*).

age nine

*"The purest affection the heart can hold
is the honest love of a nine year old."*
—Holman Francis Day

TATUM O'NEAL
appears with her father, Ryan O'Neal, in *Paper Moon*,
1973. Her role in this film earned her the Academy Award
for Best Supporting Actress. She is the youngest person
ever to receive this award.

CARL "ALFALFA" SWITZER
makes his debut in the *Our Gang* series of comedies,
1935. He became famous for singing off key, and was
the romantic interest for Darla Hood. He was killed in a
drunken brawl in 1959.

NATALIE WOOD
appears in the Christmas classic film, *Miracle on 34th
Street*, 1947.

WOLFGANG AMADEUS MOZART
astonishes his English hosts by composing "God Is Our
Refuge" while on tour in London, 1765.

FELIX MENDELSSOHN
makes his debut as a concert pianist, 1818.

age ten

"LITTLE" STEVIE WONDER
is "discovered" by Berry Gordy of Motown Records, having written his first composition, "Lonely Boy," 1960.

SHIRLEY TEMPLE
appears in *Rebecca of Sunnybrook Farm*, *Little Miss Broadway*, and *Just Around the Corner*, 1938.

YEHUDI MENUHIN
appears as a solo violinist with the New York Symphony Orchestra, 1926.

LORD KELVIN,
later a well-known British scientist, is accepted to Glasgow University in October 1834, and matriculates on November 14 (*Guinness Book of World Records*).

age eleven

ISAAC STERN
makes his debut as a solo violinist, San Francisco, 1931.

BENEDICT IX—THEOPHYLACT
is the youngest person ever elected pope, 1032 (*Guinness Book of World Records*).

age twelve

Twelve is the youngest age at which a girl in ancient Rome was allowed to marry, although most waited a year or so.

RUDOLF SERKIN
makes his concert debut as a solo pianist, 1915.

JADWIGA,
Queen of Poland, marries Jagiello, the thirty-six-year-old Duke of Lithuania, uniting their kingdoms and founding the great Jagiellonian dynasty of Poland, 1386.

WOLFGANG AMADEUS MOZART
writes his first opera, 1768.

STEVEN OF CLOYES
leads the "Children's Crusade" from France to the Holy Land, 1212. Actually the term "children's" may be a mistranslation of the Latin word *infans* meaning not only a child, but any helpless person, as the crusade included not only children, but cripples, beggars, landless peasants, and others.

RUTH LAWRENCE
is accepted to Oxford University, 1983. She graduated in 1985, at fourteen (*Guinness Book of World Records*).

CARL WITTE
receives a doctor of philosophy degree from the University of Giessen, Germany, 1814 (*Guinness Book of World Records*).

JAY LUO
graduates from Boise (Idaho) State University with a B.S. in mathematics, 1982 (*Guinness Book of World Records*).

SAMANTHA DRUCE
is the youngest woman ever to swim the English Channel, 1982 (*Guinness Book of World Records*).

age thirteen

"LITTLE" STEVIE WONDER
makes his first record, 1963.

SAMUEL GOLDFISH,
later Goldwyn, arrives from Poland in New York, 1895.
Penniless, he takes up work as an apprentice glovemaker.
Later, as a celebrated film producer, he changed his name
to Goldwyn after audiences laughed when "Goldfish"
appeared in the credits.

ANNE FRANK,
a German-Jewish girl living in Holland, begins writing
her now famous diary, 1942.

MOHANDAS GANDHI
marries Kasturbai, 1883.

CARY GRANT,
then known as Archibald Leach, runs away from home
to join an acrobatic troupe, 1917.

AKBAR THE GREAT
becomes emperor of India, 1556.

age fourteen

Although most married later, this is the earliest age at which boys in ancient Rome were allowed to marry.

BERNADETTE SOUBIROUS,
a peasant girl, sees an apparition of the Virgin Mary in a grotto at Lourdes, France, 1858.

MARY PICKFORD
uses a combination of charm and guile to land the lead role in David Belasco's play *The Warrens of Virginia*, 1907. Born Gladys Smith in Toronto, she is renamed Mary Pickford by Belasco.

age fifteen

"Standing with reluctant feet
Where the brook and river meet
Womanhood and childhood fleet."
—Henry Wadsworth Longfellow

This is the age at which Mexican-American girls celebrate their *quinceañera*, an introduction to womanhood, usually accompanied with a Mass and reception.

NADIA COMANECI
of Romania wins the Gold Medal in gymnastics at the 1976 Olympics.

LOUIS BRAILLE,
blind since age three, begins devising his alphabet for the blind, 1826.

JOE NUXHALL,
a pitcher for the Cincinnati Reds, is the youngest person ever to play major league professional baseball, 1944 (*Guinness Book of World Records*).

CHARLOTTE DOD
is the youngest tennis champion at Wimbledon, 1887 (*Guinness Book of World Records*).

VINCENT RICHARD,
playing doubles with Bill Tilden, is the youngest U.S. tennis champion, 1918 (*Guinness Book of World Records*).

age sixteen

*"Like its wars and its politicians, society has the
teenagers it deserves."*
—J. B. Priestley

MARY PICKFORD
goes to work making films for D. W. Griffith at forty
dollars per week, 1909.

CHARLES OF HABSBURG
becomes king of Spain at the height of its colonial power,
1516.

CZAR PETER,
now known as Peter the Great, consolidates his rule over
Russia by sending his half-sister into a convent, 1689.

STEVIE WONDER
has his first big hit record, "Fingertips—Part II," 1966.

DIANA ROSS
joins the Supremes, 1960.

MARGO EDEN
(born Margo Feiden) is the youngest person ever to produce a Broadway musical, *Peter Pan*, 1961 (*Guinness*).

age seventeen

"Age seventeen is the point in the journey when the parents retire to the observation car; it is the time when you stop being critical of your eldest son and he starts being critical of you."
—James and Sally Reston

DIANA ROSS
and the Supremes are signed to a recording contract with Berry Gordy's Motown Records, Detroit, 1961.

FELIX MENDELSSOHN,
already a celebrated concert pianist, composes his overture to *A Midsummer Night's Dream*, 1826. The rest of his music to Shakespeare's play was completed in 1842.

GALILEO
notices the swinging of a chandelier during an earthquake and begins his study of physics, 1581.

NATALIE WOOD
is nominated for an Academy Award for Best Supporting Actress for her role in *Rebel Without a Cause*, 1955.

STEVIE WONDER
makes the hit record "I Was Made to Love Her," 1967.

age eighteen

"I'm eighteen, I don't know what I want,"
—song by Alice Cooper, twenty-two, 1970

TUTANKHAMEN,
pharaoh of Egypt, dies c. 1357 B.C. Although a relatively
obscure monarch, he is best known as a result of Howard
Carter's discovery of his undisturbed tomb, 1922. He
came to the throne when he was about nine, and ruled
for nine years. After his death, his widow was to have
married a Hittite prince, who was killed en route to
Egypt. Therefore, he was the last of his dynasty.

QUEEN VICTORIA
takes the throne of Great Britain, 1837. Telephones,
transoceanic telegraphy, electric lights, phonographs,
motion pictures, automobiles, and antiseptic surgery were
all developed during her reign, which lasted until 1901.
She is the great-great-grandmother of the present queen,
Elizabeth II.

FRANZ JOSEF
becomes emperor of Austria, 1848, following a revolution. His reign, which lasted until his death in 1916, was
no less remarkable than Victoria's. When he came to the
throne, Austria was one of the great European powers.
Its capital, Vienna, was an important cultural center, and
Sigmund Freud, Brahms, the artist Gustav Klimt, and
Johann Strauss, Sr. and Jr., all lived there during his
reign. Johann Strauss, Jr., wrote "The Emperor Waltz"
in his honor. And yet, within only three years of Franz

19

Josef's death, his empire was divided into the states of Austria, Hungary, Czechoslovakia, and parts of Yugoslavia, Romania, the Soviet Union, Italy, and Poland.

OCTAVIAN, later CAESAR AUGUSTUS,
who may have been nineteen, is named as heir to his great-uncle Julius Caesar, 44 B.C. He became the first Roman emperor in 27 B.C., and Rome achieved her first greatness as *the* world power during his reign. He was himself a writer of some note and a patron of some of the greatest figures in Latin literature. It is said that he "found Rome stone and left it marble." The term "Augustan" is still used to describe any great period in a nation's history.

IVAN IV,
"Ivan the Terrible," becomes czar of Russia, 1547.

age nineteen

"If I knew what I thought I knew at nineteen, I would be the greatest President this country ever had."

—Warren G. Harding

CARY GRANT,
then known as Archibald Leach, begins acting in musical comedies in England, 1923.

BENITO MUSSOLINI
evades the Italian draft by fleeing to Switzerland, where he is repeatedly arrested for vagrancy and fighting, 1902. He returned to Italy to complete his military service and teach school in 1904.

LILLIAN GISH
appears in the silent film masterpiece *The Birth of a Nation*, 1915. Directed by D. W. Griffith, this was the first motion picture shown in the White House, for President and Mrs. Wilson.

CHARLES DICKENS
takes a job as a reporter in the House of Commons, 1831.

ALFRED HITCHCOCK,
better known for his future "thriller" films, goes to work in London as a technical estimator of cable for the telegraph company, 1918–19.

ANTHONY TROLLOPE,
better known today for his Barsetshire series of novels,
goes to work in the British postal service, 1834.

ETHEL WATERS
makes her stage debut as "Sweet Mama Stringbean,"
1920.

age twenty

*"Then kiss me sweet and twenty—youth's a stuff
will not endure."*
                                    —Shakespeare, *Twelfth Night*

DANIEL BOONE
is a wagon driver in Colonel Braddock's expedition to
take Fort Duquesne (now Pittsburgh) from the French.
Braddock's second-in-command is George Washington,
1755.

FEDERICO FELLINI,
famed Italian film director, directs his first film, *Variety
Lights*, 1940.

LEONARDO DA VINCI
is admitted to the Painters' Guild, 1472.

MIKE TYSON
defeats Trevor Burbick for the World Heavyweight Boxing Title, 1986.

GERTRUDE EDERLE,
an American, is the first woman to swim the English
Channel, breaking the existing men's record, 1926.

CLORIS LEACHMAN
is a runner-up in the 1946 Miss America pageant.

FIDEL CASTRO,
a student at Havana University and future revolutionary,

is given a tryout as a left-handed pitcher by the Washington Senators, 1946.

REGINALD DWIGHT
changes his name to Elton John, 1967.

CARRIE FISHER
appears as Princess Leia in *Star Wars*, 1977.

PRINCE (Rogers Nelson)
makes the album *Dirty Mind*, with some of the most risqué album lyrics to date, 1980.

DION DI MUCCI
and the Belmonts record the song "Teenager in Love," 1959.

age twenty-one

"Lightly I vaulted up four pair of stairs
In the brave days when I was twenty-one."
 —William Makepeace Thackeray

"At twenty-one, you're old enough to drink
In just a few years more, you'll be old enough to
think."

 —Anonymous

GUGLIELMO MARCONI
invents wireless telegraphy, or radio, 1895.

JEFF BRIDGES
is nominated for an Oscar for Best Supporting Actor for
The Last Picture Show, 1971. He is the son of actor Lloyd
Bridges.

BRONCO BILLY
stars in the first full-length commercial motion picture,
and the first Western, *The Great Train Robbery*, 1903.

DAVID SARNOFF
becomes a household name after he intercepts the distress signal from the H.M.S. *Titanic*, 1912. Later, he
would organize the Radio Corporation of America
(RCA).

OLIVER WENDELL HOLMES, SR.
writes the classic American poem "Old Ironsides,"
1830.

NATHAN HALE,
American Revolutionary War hero, is hanged by the British, 1776. His last words were "I regret that I have but one life to give for my country."

WAYNE GRETZKY
of the Edmonton Oilers hockey team, scores a record ninety-two goals and 212 points in the 1982 season.

ALBERT C. FULLER,
founder of the Fuller Brush Company, starts making brushes, 1906.

DWIGHT GOODEN,
a pitcher for the New York Mets, wins the 1985 Cy Young Award.

FLOYD PATTERSON
defeats Archie Moore for the World Heavyweight Boxing Championship, 1956.

BILLY THE KID,
alias William Bonney, is hanged, 1881. Born Henry McCarty in 1859, he is said to have killed one man for each of his twenty-one years.

MICK JAGGER
and the Rolling Stones record their first album, 1964.

SMOKEY ROBINSON
and the Miracles have one of their first hits, "Shop Around," 1961.

JOHN TRAVOLTA
becomes a seventies star through the television series "Welcome Back Kotter," 1975.

age twenty-two

CHARLES DARWIN
signs on as ship's naturalist on the H.M.S. *Beagle*, 1831.
His observations during this voyage were the basis for
his theory of scientific evolution.

BOB DYLAN
(born Robert Zimmerman) records his first hit record,
"Blowin' in the Wind," 1963.

JESSE OWENS
breaks three world track-and-field records and ties a
fourth—all in one day, May 25, 1935.

JOE DIMAGGIO
signs on with the New York Yankees, 1936.

SALLY STRUTHERS
appears as Gloria Stivic in the television series "All in
the Family," January 1971.

CHARLES BEST,
a medical student, working with Frederick Banting, discovers insulin, Toronto, 1921.

CYRUS MCCORMICK
first demonstrates his invention, the grain reaper, 1831.

FRIEDRICH SCHILLER,
one of the greatest names in German literature, writes *The Robbers*, a play so disturbing to the authorities that they forbid him from writing anything but medical books, 1782.

MUHAMMAD ALI HAJ,
then known as Cassius Clay, defeats Sonny Liston for the World Heavyweight Boxing Title, 1964.

JUDY GARLAND
appears in the film *Meet Me in St. Louis*, 1944.

DIANA ROSS
and the Supremes record "You Can't Hurry Love," 1966.

MICK JAGGER
and the Rolling Stones have their first number-one hit, "Satisfaction," 1965.

MARTHA REEVES
and the Vandellas record "Dancing in the Street," 1965.

OTIS WILLIAMS
and the Temptations record "The Way You Do the Things You Do," 1964.

ALICE COOPER,
although twenty-two, records his first hit, "Eighteen," 1970.

SAM COOKE
records two of his best-known hits, "You and Me," and "Chain Gang," 1957.

SAMUEL COLT
patents his new pistol, the revolver, 1836.

JOHNNY CASH
records his first hit, "Hey Porter," 1955.

ELVIS COSTELLO
(born Declan MacManus) records his first album, *My Aim Is True*, 1977.

age twenty-three

JOHN F. KENNEDY,
future president of the United States, publishes his first
book, *Why England Slept*, a study of Britain's lack of
preparation for World War II, 1940. The book was written from a unique vantage point—the author's father was
the U.S. Ambassador to Great Britain.

IRVING BERLIN
writes his first hit song, "Alexander's Ragtime Band,"
1911.

JOHANN SEBASTIAN BACH
is appointed court organist to the duke of Weimar, Germany, 1708. Although Bach was productive throughout
his life and was recognized for his skills as an organist
and composer, his works were little known, even in Germany, until after his death.

WILLIAM FAULKNER
publishes *Sartoris*, 1920. This is his first novel in the
series set in mythical "Yoknapatawpha County."

SOPHIA LOREN
marries Carlo Ponti, forty-seven, 1959.

MARTHA REEVES
and the Vandellas record the hits "Nowhere to Run,"
"I'm Ready for Love," and "Jimmy Mack," 1966.

JOHN D. ROCKEFELLER, SR.
goes into the oil business, 1862. It is interesting to note that the first commercial oil well had only been drilled in 1859, some three years earlier, and given the increased demand for petroleum products during the Civil War, Rockefeller was one of the first to exploit its potential. Ironically, Rockefeller himself, like the financier J. P. Morgan, had paid a substitute to take his place in the Union army.

GEORGE ARMSTRONG CUSTER
becomes the youngest general in the Union army, 1861, some fifteen years before he was killed at the Battle of the Little Big Horn. He was reassigned the post of colonel after the Civil War.

LEON TROTSKY,
born Lev Bronstein, escapes from Siberia, 1902. He had been sentenced there for his revolutionary activities.

DESI ARNAZ
marries Lucille Ball, 1941.

LUCILLE BALL
appears in eleven films in one year, 1934.

JULIA ROBERTS
becomes a star through the film *Pretty Woman*, 1990. A minor controversy ensued when it was learned that "body double" stand-ins were used for the nude scenes in the film.

STEVIE WONDER
is seriously injured in an automobile accident and remains in a coma for four days. Nonetheless, he won the first of three Best Album Grammy Awards (*Innervisions*) that year, 1973.

PAUL SIMON
and Art Garfunkel (born 1941) record "The Sounds of Silence," their first big hit single, 1966.

KAREEM ABDUL JABBAR
(born Lew Alcindor) is the 1970–71 National Basketball Association individual scoring champion.

ISAAC STERN
makes his Carnegie Hall debut as a solo violinist, 1943. Stern was instrumental some years later in preserving Carnegie Hall from demolition.

JOE LOUIS
defeats Jim Braddock for the World Heavyweight Boxing Championship, 1937.

age twenty-four

MUNGO PARK,
a Scottish physician and explorer, reaches the Niger River in West Africa, 1796. Park had bartered nearly all of his possessions, including the buttons off his tattered clothes, in order to feed himself on the journey.

BONNIE PARKER
of Bonnie and Clyde, is killed in a shoot-out with the law, 1934.

JOHANN STRAUSS, JR.,
Vienna's "Waltz King," combines his orchestra with that of his father, 1849, as the waltz becomes an international sensation. Their "show-stopper" was the "Radetsky March," composed by Strauss, Sr.

HERBERT HOOVER,
future president of the United States, is appointed chief engineer of the Imperial Chinese Bureau of Mines, 1898.

OLIVER WENDELL HOLMES, SR.,
now best known as a writer, begins the practice of medicine, 1835.

STEPHEN CRANE,
the son of a Methodist minister, writes an innovative psychological novel set during the Civil War, *The Red Badge of Courage*, 1895.

CAB CALLOWAY
makes his debut at New York's Cotton Club, 1931. He became famous for singing "heigh-de-ho" in such show-stopping numbers as "Minnie the Moocher," and continues performing into his eighties.

FELIX MENDELSSOHN
writes his Italian Symphony, 1833.

DOM PEDRO,
crown prince of Portugal, declares Brazil's independence from that country, naming himself emperor of Brazil, 1822. A truly remarkable man, he also wrote the Brazilian national anthem in one day and it was performed the same evening. He is probably the only reigning monarch to compose a national anthem.

JIM THORPE,
an American Indian, wins both the decathlon and pentathlon at the 1912 Olympics. He had to return his medals when it was learned that he had earned money playing minor league baseball.

ARETHA FRANKLIN
records "Respect," 1966.

VAN CLIBURN,
of the United States, wins the International Tchaikovsky Piano Competition, 1958. He received the first New York ticker-tape parade ever given a musician.

JERRY SIEGEL
launches the "Superman" cartoon series, 1938.

CLYDE TOMBAUGH,
an American astronomer, discovers the planet Pluto, 1930, in the area predicted by Percival Lowell some years earlier.

In World Heavyweight Boxing:
 JIM JEFFRIES defeats Bob Fitzsimmons, 1899;
 TOMMY BURNS defeats Marvin Hart, 1906;
 JACK DEMPSEY defeats Jess Willard, 1919;
 MAX SCHMELING defeats Jack Sharkey, 1930;
 JOE FRAZIER defeats Buster Mathis, 1968;
 GEORGE FOREMAN defeats Joe Frazier, 1973;
 JOHN TATE defeats Gerry Coetzee in fifteen rounds,
 1979; and
 MICHAEL DOKES defeats Mike Weaver, 1982.

VLADIMIR HOROWITZ
makes his American debut as a piano soloist with the
New York Philharmonic, 1928.

DIANA ROSS
and the Supremes record "I'm Gonna Make You Love
Me," 1968.

BRUCE SPRINGSTEEN
and the E Street Band record the album *The Wild, the
Innocent and the E Street Shuffle*, 1973.

PRINCE (Rogers Nelson)
makes the film *Purple Rain*, 1984.

OTIS WILLIAMS
and the Temptations record the hit single "My Girl,"
1965.

FRIEDRICH KRUPP
borrows money from his grandmother to establish the
Krupp Iron and Steel Works at Essen, Germany, 1811.
This firm became Germany's largest industrial concern
and was the major arms supplier to the kaisers and Hitler.

ISAAC NEWTON
makes his three major scientific discoveries in the space
of only eighteen months, 1665–67. The discoveries include: the nature of light and color, the theory of gravity,
and calculus. By the way, the story of an apple falling on
Newton's head, causing him to realize the law of gravity,
is a myth.

JAMES DEAN,
American actor (*Rebel Without a Cause*), is killed in an
automobile accident in California, 1955. His death produced an outpouring of emotion not seen since the death
of Rudolph Valentino. The date of his death, September
30, 1955, is the title of a 1977 film.

LEE HARVEY OSWALD
is arrested for the assassination of president John F. Kennedy, 1963. Oswald's mother said: "Lee was such a fine,
high-class boy. . . . He didn't waste his time with comic
books and trashy things. On Sundays I'd take him to
church and then we'd have lunch somewhere and go to
the zoo. If my son killed the president he would have
said so. That's the way he was brought up." (Mrs. Mar-
guerite Oswald, *Time* magazine, December 13, 1963)

LEONARD BERNSTEIN
composes his first symphony, the *Jeremiah*, 1942.

GRACIE ALLEN
marries George Burns, 31, 1927.

F. SCOTT FITZGERALD
publishes his first book, *This Side of Paradise*, 1920.

GEORGE FOX
founds the Religious Society of Friends (Quakers), 1648.

ALEXANDRE DUMAS, JR.
writes *La Dame aux Camélias*, which he later drama-
tized. This is the basis of the drama *Camille*, and Verdi's
opera *La Traviata*. It is said that the story is based on a
prostitute friend of his who used the camellia flower as
her trademark, 1848.

FRANK LLOYD WRIGHT
opens his architectural office in Chicago, 1893.

ALFRED, LORD TENNYSON
begins a ten-year silence after the death of a close friend,
1833.

WILLIAM BUTLER YEATS,
Anglo-Irish poet, is first published, 1889. Yeats's picture
appears on the Irish twenty-punt bank note.

CHARLES DICKENS
publishes his first literary work, *Sketches by Boz*, 1836.

STEVIE WONDER
wins the second of three Best Album Grammy Awards,
1974, this time for *Fulfillingness' Last Finale*.

JENNIFER JONES
wins the 1943 Best Actress Academy Award for her performance in *The Song of Bernadette*.

CHUCK YEAGER,
American test pilot, is the first human being to travel
faster than the speed of sound, 1947.

ROD CAREW,
of the Minnesota Twins, is the 1969 American League
Batting Champion, with an average of .332.

JOSE CANSECO,
of the Oakland Athletics, is chosen the American League
Most Valuable Player of 1988.

ROSE FIZGERALD,
daughter of the mayor of Boston and future mother of a
president, marries Joseph P. Kennedy, 1914.

RAY CHARLES
records his first hit single, "I've Got a Woman," 1954.

MARY TYLER MOORE
debuts as Laura Petrie in "The Dick Van Dyke Show,"
1961.

WILLIAM PITT THE YOUNGER
is chosen prime minister of Great Britain, 1783.

CALAMITY JANE,
born Martha Jane Canary, arrives in Deadwood, South
Dakota, 1876, boasting of her adventures.

GIOACCHINO ROSSINI,
Italian composer, writes his best-known opera, *Il Bar-
biere di Siviglia*, 1816.

age twenty-five

QUEEN ELIZABETH II,
queen of Great Britain (and Canada), born April 21, 1926,
becomes queen upon the death of her father, King George
VI, in February 1952.

CLYDE BARROW
of Bonnie and Clyde is killed in a shoot-out with the law,
1934. One of the things that made him a legend during
the depression was his practice of burning all unrecorded
mortgages during bank robberies.

MARTIN LUTHER KING, JR.,
becomes pastor of the Dexter Avenue Baptist Church in
Montgomery, Alabama, 1954.

JOSEPH P. KENNEDY, SR.,
becomes the youngest bank president in the United States,
1913.

ANNIE OAKLEY,
famous sharpshooter, joins Buffalo Bill's Wild West
Show, 1885. She performed for Queen Victoria, and once
shot a cigarette out of the mouth of future Kaiser Wilhelm II of Germany at his request.

ERNEST HEMINGWAY
publishes his first book, *In Our Time*, 1924.

ERIC CLAPTON
makes his first solo album, 1970.

CHARLOTTE CORDAY
stabs Jean Marat in his bathtub, 1792. She had made two
unsuccessful attempts to see him and stabbed him on the
third. This is the subject of David's famous painting *Marat Stabbed in the Bathtub*. It is also the basis of *Marat/Sade*, a play in which the stabbing is reenacted by
residents of the insane asylum at Charenton under the
direction of the Marquis de Sade.

JOSEPH SMITH
establishes the Church of Jesus Christ of Latter-Day
Saints ("Mormons"), 1830.

BOOKER T. WASHINGTON
becomes president of Tuskegee University, 1881.

MUHAMMAD ALI HAJ,
World Heavyweight Boxing Champion, is convicted of
draft evasion during the Vietnam War, 1967. Ali, a black
Muslim, claimed conscientious objector status, and the
conviction was later overturned.

GEORGE JORGENSEN
becomes CHRISTINE JORGENSEN in the first sex-change operation, Denmark, 1952.

DARRYL ZANUCK
produces the first commercial sound motion picture, *The
Jazz Singer*, 1927.

DAVID BOWIE
makes the album *Hunky Dory*, including the hit single
"Changes," 1972.

ROD STEWART
and his band, Faces, make an American tour, 1970.

ELTON JOHN
records the hit album *Honky Chateau*, 1972.

DAVID BYRNE
and the band Talking Heads record their first hit single,
"Psycho Killer," 1977.

LEVI STUBBS
and the Four Tops record "Baby I Need Your Loving,"
1964.

FRANKIE VALLI
and the Four Seasons record their hit single "Sherry,"
1962.

SMOKEY ROBINSON
and the Miracles record two big hit singles, "Ooh, Baby,
Baby," and "The Tracks of My Tears," 1965.

OTIS WILLIAMS
and the Temptations record "I'm Gonna Make You Love
Me," with Diana Ross and the Supremes, 1969.

MICKEY MANTLE
has an excellent year, 1956. He is chosen the American
League Most Valuable Player, leads the American League
in home runs (fifty-two), runs batted in (130), and has
the highest batting average in the league. Playing for the
New York Yankees, he led the league in home runs in
1955, 1956, 1958, and 1960. He was chosen American
League MVP in 1956, 1957, and 1962.

WADE BOGGS
is the American League's top batter, 1983.

GEORGE WESLEY BELLOWS,
an American painter, paints the classic view of underworld life, *Stag at Sharkey's*—an illegal boxing match,
1906.

In World Heavyweight Boxing:
   MAX BAER defeats Primo Carnera in an eleventh-
   round knockout, 1934;
   FLOYD PATTERSON defeats Ingemar Johannson,
   1960;
   LEON SPINKS defeats Muhammad Ali after fifteen
   rounds, 1978 (but not for long); and
   GREG PAGE defeats Gerry Coetzee, 1984.

CHARLES A. LINDBERGH
makes the first transatlantic solo airplane flight, 1927.
Ironically, aviation authorities had nearly grounded him
only months before for reckless flying.

MICHAEL JACKSON
wins three 1983 Grammy Awards, including Best Album
(*Thriller*), Best Record (''Beat It''), and Best Male Pop
Vocalist.

ALEXANDER GRAHAM BELL,
future inventor of the telephone, establishes a school for
the deaf, Boston, 1872.

ROBERT RIPLEY
launches his ''Ripley's Believe It or Not'' cartoon series,
1918.

HIROHITO
becomes emperor of Japan, 1926.

EDWARD WHYMPER,
an Englishman, is the first to climb Switzerland's Matterhorn, 1865.

VLADIMIR I. LENIN
is arrested for revolutionary activity and sentenced to Siberia, 1895.

JOHANN WOLFGANG VON GOETHE,
perhaps the greatest name in German literature, publishes his first work, *The Sorrows of Young Werther*, an international best-seller, 1774. The book, a poetic treatment of unrequited love, allegedly sparked a wave of suicides and is the basis for Massenet's opera *Westhes*.

age twenty-six

ROBERT CLIVE
leads British and Indian troops to capture the French fort at Arcot, India, 1751. This was the beginning of British colonial rule in India, which would be firmly established a century later.

NICHOLAS II
becomes czar of Russia, 1894. The last of the czars, Nicholas was deposed by the Bolsheviks (Communists) during the 1917 Russian Revolution. During World War I, he was an ally of his first cousin George V of Great Britain, against their mutual first cousin Kaiser Wilhelm II of Germany. All were grandchildren of Queen Victoria.

ALBERT EINSTEIN,
a Swiss patent office inspector and part-time theoretical physicist, publishes the "Theory of Relativity," 1905.

VALENTINA TERESHKOVA
of the Soviet Union is the first woman to travel in outer space, 1963.

EDMUND HALLEY
successfully predicts the 1683 return of the comet now named for him.

NAPOLEON BONAPARTE
marries Josephine Beauharnais, thirty-two, 1795.

ABRAHAM LINCOLN's
business partner, George F. Berry, dies, 1835. Lincoln
was then personally liable for $1,100 in debts, an enor-
mous sum at the time.

LOUIS PASTEUR
is recognized for his studies of the structures of crystals,
1848.

PETER ILYICH TCHAIKOVSKY
begins teaching harmony at the Moscow Conservatory of
Music, 1866.

JEAN HARLOW,
1930s sex symbol, dies, 1936.

VIVIEN LEIGH,
an Englishwoman, appears as Scarlett O'Hara in *Gone
With the Wind*, for which she wins the 1939 Academy
Award for Best Actress.

NAT KING COLE
signs a recording contract with Capitol Records, 1943.

MADONNA (CICCONE)
becomes famous with the release of her hit recording
"Like a Virgin," 1984. (Both Madonna and the author
of *The Book of Ages* are natives of Bay City, Michigan.)

WILL ROGERS
makes his New York stage debut as a comedian and lariat
artist, 1905.

ELLA FITZGERALD
sets out on a solo career, 1942.

AUBREY BEARDSLEY,
English pen-and-ink illustrator and pioneer of the art nouveau style, dies, 1898. At the time of his death, Beardsley, a devout Roman Catholic, felt great remorse for the erotic nature of some of his work. His work again became very popular in the 1970s.

ORSON WELLES,
American actor, writer, producer, and director, makes the film *Citizen Kane*, based on the life of newspaper magnate William Randolph Hearst, 1940. This film is now considered one of the greatest American films ever made.

STEVIE WONDER
wins the third of three Grammy Awards for Best Album, this time for *Songs in the Key of Life*, 1976.

JOHN WILKES BOOTH
shoots President Abraham Lincoln at Ford's Theater, Washington, on Good Friday, April 13, 1865. Booth leaped to the stage and shouted *Sic semper tyrannis* (Latin: "Thus ever to tyrants")—the motto of the state of Virginia.

PABLO PICASSO
paints *Les Demoiselles d'Avignon*, 1907. This marks a departure from his earlier Blue Period paintings.

BARBRA STREISAND
shares the 1968 Academy Award for Best Actress with Katharine Hepburn after a tie vote. Streisand had been nominated for her performance in the film *Funny Girl*.

JOHN PHILIP SOUSA,
the American "March King," organizes his first band, 1880.

WAYNE GRETZKY
wins his seventh consecutive Hart Trophy—hockey's most valuable player award, 1987, while playing for the Edmonton Oilers. He also won the 1981–87 Ross Trophies (for leading scorer in professional hockey) while playing for Edmonton, as well as in 1990, while playing for the Los Angeles Kings. He also won the 1980 Lady Byng Trophy (for most gentlemanly player) and the Conn Smythe Trophy (most valuable player in the NHL playoffs) in 1985 and 1988.

LEVI STUBBS
and the Four Tops record the hit "I Can't Help Myself (Sugar Pie, Honey Bunch)," 1965.

BOB MARLEY
and the Wailers record *Catch a Fire*, 1972. This album was an important part of the growing popularity of Jamaican reggae music in the United States and Canada.

RAINIER
becomes prince of Monaco, 1949.

GRACE KELLY,
later Princess Grace of Monaco, wins the 1954 Best Actress Academy Award for *The Country Girl*.

LIZA MINNELLI
wins the 1972 Best Actress Academy Award for *Cabaret*. She is the daughter of actress Judy Garland and director Vincente Minnelli.

MARCEL DUCHAMP
creates a controversy with his painting *Nude Descending a Staircase*, 1913—an important moment in the history of modern art.

VELASQUEZ
becomes court painter to King Philip IV of Spain, 1625.

JOHANN FRIEDRICH BOETTGER,
a potter of Meissen, Germany, solves an important problem, 1708. For centuries, Europeans had imported porcelain from China at exorbitant prices and had failed to discover the secret of making it. Boettger was the first European to produce porcelain.

BRUCE SPRINGSTEEN
records *Born to Run*, and is the first person to have his picture on the cover of both *Time* and *Newsweek* simultaneously in one week, the week of October 27, 1975.

In World Heavyweight Boxing:
    JIM CORBETT defeats John L. Sullivan in twenty-one rounds, 1892;
    PRIMO CARNERA defeats Jack Sharkey, 1933;
    INGEMAR JOHANNSON defeats Floyd Patterson, 1959;
    JOE FRAZIER defeats Jimmy Ellis, 1970;
    TIM WITHERSPOON defeats Greg Page in twelve rounds, 1984; and
    TONY TUBBS defeats Greg Page, 1985.

age twenty-seven

"She was a faded, but still lovely woman of twenty-seven."

—F. Scott Fitzgerald
(written when he was twenty-four)

JAKOB GRIMM
and his younger brother Wilhelm publish *Die Märchen der Brüder Grimm* (*Grimms' Fairy Tales*), 1812. The more serious work of the brothers was linguistics, and they developed Grimm's Law, which governs the consonant shifts between different languages in the Indo-European language group.

WALT DISNEY
makes the first Mickey Mouse cartoon, "Steamboat Willie," 1928. Disney had earlier gone bankrupt trying to develop animated film.

QUEEN CHRISTINA
of Sweden shocks her Lutheran subjects by converting to Roman Catholicism and abdicates, 1654.

GUGLIELMO MARCONI
makes the first successful transatlantic wireless telegraphic (radio) transmission between Poldhu, Cornwall (Great Britain), and Newfoundland, 1901.

CAPTAIN MATTHEW WEBB
is the first person to swim the English Channel, 1875. He covered forty miles in twenty-two hours.

BESSIE SMITH,
the "Empress of the Blues," makes her first record for
Capitol, 1923. Her housekeeper went on to fame in her
own right under the name Billie Holiday.

JOANNE WOODWARD
wins the 1957 Best Actress Academy Award for *The Three
Faces of Eve*, a study of schizophrenia.

DAVID LIVINGSTONE,
Scottish explorer and medical missionary, sails for Africa, 1840.

SOPHIA LOREN
wins the 1961 Best Actress Academy Award for *Two
Women*.

MARGARET MEAD,
American anthropologist, publishes the landmark work
Coming of Age in Samoa, 1928.

YUL BRYNNER,
later famous as an actor, is a French-language broad-
caster for the U.S. Office of War Information, 1942.

GEORGE BRETT,
third baseman for the Kansas City Royals, is chosen as
the American League Most Valuable Player, 1980.

SERGEI EISENSTEIN,
one of the greatest Soviet filmmakers, makes the silent
masterpiece *The Battleship Potemkin*, 1926. The film,
considered one of the greatest ever made, is an account
of a mutiny of sailors during the aborted 1905 revolution.

ABRAHAM LINCOLN
is licensed to practice law in Illinois, 1836.

HUGH HEFNER
publishes the first edition of *Playboy*, 1954.

BETTE DAVIS
wins the 1935 Best Actress Academy Award for *Dangerous*.

COUNT GALEAZZO CIANO
marries the boss's daughter, Edda Mussolini, 1930. However, his father-in-law, Benito Mussolini, later had him executed.

HENRY DAVID THOREAU
moves to Walden Pond, where he meditates and works at odd jobs, 1834. This is where he developed his classic book, *Walden*.

KAREN BLACK
portrays an LSD-tripping prostitute in the film *Easy Rider*, 1969.

SIR ISAAC NEWTON
publishes his studies of calculus, 1669.

ROD CAREW
is the 1972 American League Batting Champion, with an average of .318.

WADE BOGGS,
of the Boston Red Sox, is the 1987 American League Batting Champion, with an average of .368.

MARY PICKFORD
plays the role of a twelve-year-old girl in the silent film *Pollyanna*, 1920.

ERNEST HEMINGWAY
publishes *The Sun Also Rises*, 1926.

EDWARD M. GALLAUDET
founds Gallaudet College in Washington, D.C., 1864.
This is the first college for the deaf in America.

RICHARD DREYFUSS
appears in the film *Jaws*, 1975.

JUAN BELMONTE,
one of Spain's greatest bullfighters, kills 200 bulls in 109
bullfights in one year, 1919.

ALOIS SENEFELDER
invents the lithograph, 1798.

GIORGIO DE CHIRICO
is conscripted into the Italian army, 1915. Later, he suffers a nervous breakdown and develops his "metaphysi-
cal" style of painting, an important influence on modern
art. He is considered a forerunner of surrealism.

GEORGE CLINTON,
father of "funk" music, and the Parliaments record "I
Just Wanna Testify," 1967.

BOB MARLEY
and the Wailers record the album *Burnin'*, 1973.

DONNA SUMMER
records the quintessential 1970s sexually oriented disco
hit, "I Love to Love You Baby," 1976.

DAVID BOWIE
records the album *Diamond Dogs*, 1974.

SMOKEY ROBINSON
and the Miracles record the hit single "I Second That
Emotion," 1967.

FRANK SINATRA
is selected *Billboard*'s 1943 Top Male Vocalist.

JIM MORRISON
of the Doors dies in a bathtub in Paris, July 3, 1971. The
official death certificate listed the cause as a heart attack.

"Country" JOE MCDONALD
and the Fish appear at the Woodstock Festival, 1969.

NIKOLAI GOGOL
establishes himself as an important Russian writer with
the publication of the satirical play *The Inspector General*, 1836.

JACK LONDON
publishes *The Call of the Wild*, 1903.

NEIL YOUNG
records the album *Harvest*, 1972.

GEORGES SEURAT
establishes himself and his technique, "pointillism" with
the painting *Sunday Afternoon on the Island of the Grand
Jatte*, 1886, the inspiration for Sondheim and Lapine's
play *Sunday in the Park with George*.

JANIS JOPLIN
dies of a heroin overdose, 1970.

In World Heavyweight Boxing:
    EZZARD CHARLES defeats "Jersey Joe" Walcott in
    fifteen rounds, 1949; and
    MIKE WEAVER defeats John Tate with a fifteenth
    round knockout, 1980.

age twenty-eight

*"A woman deserves to have more than twelve years
between twenty-eight and forty."*
　　　　　　　　　　　　　　　　—James Thurber

ANDREW CARNEGIE
enters the iron and steel business, 1864.

IGOR STRAVINSKY
composes his famous *Firebird* suite, 1910.

ROBERT RAUSCHENBERG,
American artist, creates a stir when he erases a drawing
by Willem de Kooning and retitles it *Erased de Kooning
Drawing*, 1953.

LUDWIG ZAMENHOF,
a Polish opthalmologist, invents the most successful of
artificial languages, Esperanto, 1887. Based on elements
from the Germanic and Romance language families, it
has a simple grammar with no exceptions. As of 1991,
Swiss Radio International has regularly scheduled broadcasts in Esperanto.

LUDWIG VAN BEETHOVEN
realizes that he is losing his hearing, 1798.

STEVEN AUSTIN
organizes 100 American families to establish a colony in
the Mexican province of Texas, 1821.

CLEOPATRA,
"Queen of the Nile," meets the Roman Marc Antony and they become lovers. Later, she has a son by Julius Caesar, c. 50 B.C.

SIR ARTHUR CONAN DOYLE,
a physician, writes *A Study in Scarlet*, the first of his Sherlock Holmes stories, 1887.

WILLIAM SHAKESPEARE
is recognized for his abilities as an actor and playwright, after the success of *Henry VI*, 1592.

MARILYN MONROE
marries Joe DiMaggio, 1954.

COUNT LEO TOLSTOY,
Russian novelist, retires from the army to pursue the life of a writer and gentleman farmer, 1856.

CASIMIR FUNK,
a Polish chemist living in England, discovers vitamins, 1912.

JOSEPH STALIN,
a seminary dropout, robs the Russian State Bank Transport to help finance the Bolshevik party, 1907.

BILL HALEY
and the Comets record "Rock Around the Clock," 1955.

BETTE MIDLER,
the "Divine Miss M," is named Best New Performer of 1972 at the Grammy Awards.

PAUL MCCARTNEY
files a suit to have the Beatles disbanded, 1970.

UPTON SINCLAIR
creates a national sensation with his book *The Jungle*, an exposé of corruption, filth, and dangerous labor practices in the meat-packing industry, 1906.

FREDERICK THE GREAT,
king of Prussia, begins his reign by invading Silesia, 1740.

DUKE ELLINGTON
is the featured performer at New York's Cotton Club, 1927.

JACKIE ROBINSON
becomes the first black to play major league professional baseball, 1947.

MERLE HAGGARD,
country-and-western music star, who had been released from prison only five years earlier, is signed to a recording contract with Capitol Records, 1965.

ELIZABETH TAYLOR
wins the 1960 Best Actress Academy Award for *Butterfield Eight*.

DOM PEDRO,
having made himself emperor of Brazil only four years earlier, finds himself also king of Portugal—the country from which he declared Brazil independent—upon the death of his father, 1826.

SID CAESAR
stars in the television classic "Your Show of Shows," 1950.

DOUGLAS FAIRBANKS, SR.,
the motion picture industry's first "swashbuckler,"
makes his first film, *The Lamb*, in 1915.

JIMI HENDRIX
dies, 1970.

MAGIC JOHNSON
is the NBA Most Valuable Player, 1987. He was also
voted MVP in the playoffs for 1980, 1982, and 1987.

In World Heavyweight Boxing:
  GENE TUNNEY defeats Jack Dempsey, 1926;
  SONNY LISTON knocks out Floyd Patterson, 1962;
  JIMMY ELLIS defeats Jerry Quarry in fifteen rounds,
  1968;
  LARRY HOLMES defeats Ken Norton in fifteen
  rounds, 1978;
  GERRY COETZEE defeats Michael Dokes, 1983; and
  TIM WITHERSPOON defeats Tony Tubbs in fifteen
  rounds, 1986.

ANDRE JACQUES GARNERIN
is the first person to jump from a hot-air balloon with a
parachute, 1797.

CHARLES SCHULTZ
launches the "Peanuts" cartoon series, 1950.

PAMELA TRAVERS
of Australia writes *Mary Poppins*, 1934.

JUAN TERRY TRIPPE
establishes Pan American World Airways, 1927.

SIR FRANK WHITTLE's
patents on the turbojet airplane engine lapse because he
doesn't have the money for the filing fee, 1935.

MARVIN HAMLISCH

is the first person ever to win three Academy Awards in one night, 1974. He won one for the musical score of *The Sting*, a second for the musical score of *The Way We Were*, and a third for the title song of the latter.

age twenty-nine

"Gather ye rosebuds while ye may
 Old time is still aflying
And this same flower that smiles today
 Tomorrow will be dying . . .
Then be not coy, but use your time
 and while ye may go marry.
For having lost but once your prime
 You may forever tarry."
                              —Robert Herrick

"I have never admitted that I am more than twenty-nine, or thirty at the most. Twenty-nine when there are pink shades, thirty when there are not."
        —Oscar Wilde, *Lady Windermere's Fan*

"That air of superiority over the rest of the world which usually disappears once the twenties have been passed."
            —Ivan Turgenev, *Fathers and Sons*

BUDDHA,
a wealthy Indian prince, leaves his family and considerable property to search for eternal truth, c. 300 B.C..

ST. FRANCIS OF ASSISI
establishes the Franciscan monastic order, 1210.

WILHELM II
becomes kaiser of Germany, 1888.

LARRY BIRD
of the Boston Celtics is the NBA Most Valuable Player for the second year in a row, 1985.

MEL BLANC,
the "Man of a Thousand Voices," including Bugs Bunny,
Sylvester the Cat, Yosemite Sam, Barney Rubble (of
"The Flintstones"), the sound of Jack Benny's car, and
many, many others, goes to work in the cartoon department at Warner Brothers, 1937.

VICTOR HUGO
writes the novel *Hunchback of Notre Dame* in only four
months, 1831.

JOHN F. KENNEDY
is first elected to Congress, 1946.

RONALD REAGAN
marries Jane Wyman, 1940.

MARIO ANDRETTI
wins the 1969 Indianapolis 500.

J. EDGAR HOOVER
is appointed director of the U.S. Federal Bureau of Investigation, 1924.

ERSKINE CALDWELL
writes *Tobacco Road*, 1932.

E. M. FORSTER,
celebrated English novelist, writes *A Room with a View*,
1908.

ERIC CLAPTON,
having conquered his heroin addiction, makes a dramatic
comeback with the release of his album *461 Ocean Bou-
levard*, 1974.

FLORENCE GRIFFITH JOYNER
retires from track and field, 1989. She had won three Gold Medals and one Silver at the 1988 Olympics in addition to holding the women's world track records for the one hundred-meter and two hundred-meter runs.

JULIE ANDREWS
wins the 1964 Best Actress Academy Award for *Mary Poppins*.

THOMAS EDISON,
not quite thirty, patents the phonograph, 1877.

ALEXANDER GRAHAM BELL
patents the telephone, 1876. (Both Bell and Edison were born in 1847.)

OGDEN NASH
publishes his first book of verse, *Hard Lines*, 1931.

THOMAS WOLFE
publishes *Look Homeward Angel*, 1929.

FRANCIS FORD COPPOLA
directs *Finian's Rainbow*, 1968.

TED WILLIAMS
of the Boston Red Sox, is the 1947 American League Batting champion, with an average of .343.

DIANA ROSS
appears in the film, and records the album, *Lady Sings the Blues*, a biographical film about the life of Billie Holiday, 1973.

HOAGY CARMICHAEL
quits the practice of law to become a full-time songwriter, 1928.

RED ROSA,
born Claire Lacomb, is arrested by the French Revolutionary authorities for inciting the women of Paris to demand equal rights, 1794. Thus, *"Liberté, egalité, fraternité"* were apparently extended to French men only.

GEORGIA O'KEEFE,
American painter, first exhibits her works at the 219 Gallery in New York, 1916.

NICOLA SACCO
and Bartolomeo Vanzetti, thirty-two, are accused of killing two during a Massachusetts bank robbery, despite circumstantial evidence and political overtones, as the two were suspected anarchists, 1921. Prior to their execution six years later, there was an international outcry protesting their innocence. In 1977, Massachusetts governor Michael Dukakis signed a proclamation exonerating them.

ROD CAREW
is the 1974 American League Batting Champion, with an average of .364.

RAY CHARLES
has his first million-selling record, "What I'd Say," 1959.

ANDREAS VESALIUS,
"Father of Anatomy," publishes the first modern scientific treatment of the subject *Concerning the Fabric of the Human Body*, 1543.

RUDYARD KIPLING
writes *The Jungle Book*, 1894.

AARON MONTGOMERY WARD
goes into the mail-order catalog business, 1872.

RICHARD DREYFUSS
appears in *Close Encounters of the Third Kind*, 1977. That same year, he won the Academy Award for Best Actor for *The Goodbye Girl*.

SOREN KIERKEGAARD
Danish philosopher and precursor of existentialism, writes *Fear and Trembling*, 1842.

EDMOND ROSTAND
writes *Cyrano de Bergerac*, 1897.

MARC BOLAN
of the band T. Rex is killed in an automobile accident, 1977.

CHUCK BERRY,
months before his thirtieth birthday, records the hit "Johnny B. Goode," 1956.

HANK WILLIAMS, SR.
dies on New Year's Eve, 1953.

OTIS WILLIAMS
and the Temptations record "Ball of Confusion," 1970.

ANTONIO GAUDI
begins work on the Church of the Holy Family, Barcelona, 1882. As of this writing, his building plans have still not been completely executed.

BETH HENLEY,
American playwright, wins the 1981 Pulitzer Prize for *Crimes of the Heart*.

age thirty

"Never trust anyone over thirty."
— John Lennon (at age twenty-seven)

"The only time you really live fully is from thirty to sixty . . . the young are slaves to dreams; the old, servants of regret. Only the middle-aged have all their five senses in the keeping of their wits."
— Hervey Allen (1889–1948)

"It is well for the world that, in most of us, by the age of thirty, the character has set like plaster and will never soften again."
— William James (1842–1910)

"The man of virtue and talent, who should die in his thirtieth year is, with regard to his own feelings, longer than a miserable . . . slave who dreams out a century of goodness.
— Percy Bysshe Shelley

JESUS CHRIST
begins his ministry, c. A.D. 24.

HENRY FORD
builds his first gasoline engine, 1893.

CHARLES DICKENS
visits the United States and Canada, 1842.

DAVID
becomes king of Israel, c. 1000 B.C.

JOSEPH BRAMAH
of England invents the modern water closet (i.e., loo, toilet), 1778. (Author's note: When one is over thirty, one appreciates such comforts.)

OMAR SHARIF
makes his American film debut in *Lawrence of Arabia*, 1962.

HANS CHRISTIAN ANDERSEN,
desperately in need of money, publishes four fairy tales, Denmark, 1835.

SIR FREDERICK BANTING,
with a team including Charles Best, discovers insulin, Toronto, 1921.

TED WILLIAMS
of the Boston Red Sox is the 1948 American League Batting Champion, with an average of .369.

KARL MARX
writes the *Communist Manifesto*, 1848.

CASIMIR III
becomes King of Poland, 1340. He was probably the most enlightened European ruler of the time, a protector of the Jews and a patron of the arts and sciences.

ERNEST HEMINGWAY
publishes *A Farewell to Arms*, 1929.

ERSKINE CALDWELL
writes *God's Little Acre*, 1933.

BOB HOPE
stars in the 1933 musical comedy *Roberta*.

SIR LAURENCE OLIVIER
has his first stage success as *Hamlet*, at London's Old
Vic Theatre, 1937.

BARBARA BRADEN
(''The Girls'') is the first black female cartoonist to appear in a major metropolitan daily, the *Detroit Free Press*,
1989.

JULIE ANDREWS
appears in the film *The Sound of Music*, 1965.

SIDNEY REILLY,
(born Sigmund G. Rosenblum in Russia), goes to work
for the British Secret Intelligence Service, 1904. His
exploits are the basis of the BBC television series
''Reilly—Ace of Spies.''

MANOLETE,
considered by some Spaniards to be the greatest bull-
fighter of all time, is gored to death on the eve of his
retirement, 1947.

ALTHEA GIBSON
wins both Wimbledon and the U.S. Singles Championship, 1957. She is the first black tennis champion in either category.

THOMAS GALLAUDET,
father of the founder of Washington's Gallaudet College,
introduces sign language to America, 1817.

TOSHIRO MIFUNE,
a Japanese actor sometimes called the ''Japanese John
Wayne,'' appears in the Akira Kurosawa classic film
Rashomon, 1950.

CLAUDE CHAPPE
of France invents semaphore signals, one of the most important pretelegraphic forms of communication at sea, 1793.

BENJAMIN WEST,
an American painter working in Britain, is a founder-member of the British Royal Academy, 1768.

INGRID BERGMAN
stars in *Casablanca*, 1942. This film won the 1943 Best Picture and Best Director (Michael Curtiz) Academy Awards.

JACK JOHNSON
becomes the first black World Heavyweight Boxing Champion, 1908.

WOODY ALLEN
makes his debut as a screenwriter and actor in *What's New Pussycat?*, 1965.

ROD CAREW
is the 1975 American League Batting Champ for the fifth time, with an average of .359.

KNUTE ROCKNE,
a Norwegian Protestant, becomes head football coach at Notre Dame University, 1918.

EMILY BRONTE
writes *Wuthering Heights*, 1848.

GURU NANAK
of the Punjab (a region in India-Pakistan) has a profound religious experience that results in the founding of the Sikh religion, 1499.

JOHN LENNON and RINGO STARR
were thirty when the Beatles disbanded, 1970.

SANDY KOUFAX
pitches a perfect game, Los Angeles vs. Chicago (1-0),
September 9, 1965.

WARREN BEATTY
becomes a major film star in *Bonnie and Clyde*, 1967.

ISAAC HAYES
wins both an Academy Award and a Grammy for "The
Theme from *Shaft*," 1972.

CHUCK BERRY
records the hit single "Maybelline," 1956.

ELLIOTT GOULD
has a turnaround thirtieth year. Gould had a virtually
impossible time establishing himself as an actor and
worked as an elevator operator and vacuum cleaner salesman among other jobs. At twenty-five, he married Barbra
Streisand, and although her career was phenomenal, his
appeared to go nowhere fast. He was deeply hurt by ref-
erences to him as "Mr. Streisand," underwent psycho-
analysis, and suffered from severe depression. Then, at
thirty, he appeared in *The Night They Raided Minsky's*,
1968. The next year, he was nominated for an Academy
Award for *Bob and Carol and Ted and Alice*.

GENE HACKMAN
makes his first appearance on film in a bit part in *Mad
Dog Call*, 1961.

age thirty-one

ADOLF HITLER
addresses two thousand followers at the Munich Hofbrauhaus, 1920.

ELEUTHERE IRENEE DUPONT
selects Wilmington, Delaware, as the site of the new gunpowder mill, the beginning of the Dupont Chemical Corporation, 1802.

CHARLES DICKENS
publishes the immediate best-seller *A Christmas Carol*, 1843.

RAPHAEL
is appointed Chief Architect of St. Peter's Church, Rome, by Pope Leo X, 1514.

LOUISA MAY ALCOTT
publishes *Little Women*, 1863.

IGOR STRAVINSKY
composes the ballet *Le Sacre du Printemps* ("The Rite of Spring"), 1913.

EDOUARD MANET,
celebrated French painter, shocks Paris with his nude painting *Olympia*, 1863. Outraged patrons ordered it removed from the gallery.

ERICH MARIA REMARQUE
writes *All's Quiet on the Western Front*, 1929.

JOHN DILLINGER,
"Public Enemy Number One," is gunned down by the
FBI near Mercer, Wisconsin, 1934.

JULIUS ERVING
is the NBA's Most Valuable Player of 1981.

REGGIE JACKSON
hits five home runs in the 1977 World Series—a record.

JOHN D. ROCKEFELLER, SR.
organizes Standard Oil, 1870.

FLETCHER HENDERSON's
career as a jazz pioneer seems over as he suffers serious
head injuries in a 1928 automobile accident.

SIR CHRISTOPHER WREN
designs the Sheldonian Theatre in London, establishing
himself as an important architect, 1633. His most important work was St. Paul's Cathedral.

JACK DEMPSEY
loses the World Heavyweight Boxing Title to Gene Tunney, 1926.

JOHN HERSEY
wins a 1945 Pulitzer Prize for *A Bell for Adano*.

CHEVY CHASE,
almost thirty-two, appears in television's "Saturday Night
Live," 1975.

ALLAN PINKERTON,
an immigrant from Scotland, establishes the first detective agency in the United States, 1850.

CHESTER GOULD
creates the cartoon strip "Dick Tracy," 1931.

ARTURO TOSCANINI
is named principal conductor of the La Scala Opera in Milan, 1898.

AGNES CAMPBELL MCPHAIL
is the first woman elected to the Canadian Parliament, 1921.

EDWARD BULWER-LYTTON
writes *The Last Days of Pompeii*, 1834.

JOHN LENNON's
"Imagine" is the number-one song on the charts in the United States, 1971.

CYNDI LAUPER
makes her debut album, *She's So Unusual*, 1984.

DAVID BYRNE
and Talking Heads make the *Speaking in Tongues* album, 1983.

BO DIDDLEY,
rhythm-and-blues pioneer, records "Say Man," 1959. He was born Elias Bates McDaniel and took his name from an African musical instrument.

GEORGES SEURAT,
French artist, dies from meningitis, 1891.

CHARLES WESLEY,
who, along with his brother John, is considered a founder of Methodism, undergoes a profound religious awakening, which his brother experiences three days later, 1738.

LOUIS LUMIERE
and his brother Auguste patent the motion picture projector, 1895.

JAMES CAGNEY
makes his first hit movie as a gangster in *The Public Enemy*, 1931.

BILLY GRAHAM
holds his first evangelistic crusade, Los Angeles, 1949.

MAXIMILIAN SCHELL,
a native of Austria, wins the 1961 Best Actor Academy Award for playing a Nazi on trial in *Judgment at Nuremberg*.

JAWAHARLAL NEHRU,
future prime minister of India, is imprisoned by the British for his nationalist activities for the first time, 1921.

SCOTT JOPLIN,
a black American composer, writes the classic ''Maple Leaf Rag,'' 1899.

PIERRE JOSEPHE PROUDHON,
French socialist, writes *Property Is Theft*, 1840.

EDVARD GRIEG,
Norway's greatest composer, writes the *Peer Gynt Suite* at the request of Norway's greatest playwright, Henrik Ibsen, 1874.

age thirty-two

ALEXANDER THE GREAT
dies after overindulging himself at a victory party in Babylon, 323 B.C.

MAXIMILIEN ROBESPIERRE
is elected to the French Revolutionary Council of Public Safety—a misnomer if ever there was one, given its bloodthirsty nature—and directs the Reign of Terror, 1793. He himself was guillotined a year later.

LUDWIG VAN BEETHOVEN
composes the *Moonlight* Sonata, 1802.

CLAUDE DEBUSSY,
who had applied impressionism to music, gets terrible reviews from the critics for *The Afternoon of a Faun*, 1894.

JULIUS ROSENBERG
and his wife Ethel, twenty-nine, are arrested on charges of espionage for the Soviet Union while they are at home listening to ''The Lone Ranger'' on the radio, 1950.

WILLIAM RANDOLPH HEARST
buys *The New York Journal*, 1895.

GWENDOLYN BROOKS
is the first African-American writer to win a Pulitzer Prize, 1950. She won for her book *Annie Allen*.

SIR ARTHUR CONAN DOYLE,
now famous for his Sherlock Holmes stories, quits the practice of medicine to write full-time, 1891.

MUHAMMAD ALI HAJ
reclaims the World Heavyweight Boxing Title by defeating George Foreman in Zaire, 1974.

STEVE ALLEN
hosts the first "Tonight Show" on NBC television, 1954.

ORVILLE WRIGHT
and his brother Wilbur, twenty-six, successfully fly their airplane at Kitty Hawk, North Carolina, 1903.

RICHARD STRAUSS,
German composer, writes *Thus Spake Zarathustra*, based on the writings of philosopher Friedrich Nietzsche. The music is probably best known to contemporary audiences from the film score of *2001: A Space Odyssey*.

JAMES STEWART
wins the 1940 Best Actor Academy Award for *The Philadelphia Story*.

ULYSSES S. GRANT,
future president of the United States, is forced to resign from the army due to his drinking problem, 1854.

AL CAPONE
is sentenced to eleven years in federal prison for income tax evasion, 1931.

THOMAS A. EDISON
invents the incandescent electric light, 1879.

CLIFFORD BEERS
writes *The Mind That Found Itself*, 1908. This moving
story describes how Beers had been institutionalized for
mental illness and suffered physical abuse. He recovered
from mental illness and became a pioneer in the mental
health movement.

MARJORIE LAWRENCE,
an Australian Wagnerian soprano, develops polio, 1941.
Although it looked like the end of her career, she underwent therapy with Sister Elizabeth Kenny and resumed
her promising career. This was the basis of the 1955 film
Interrupted Melody starring Eleanor Parker, with singing
dubbed by Eileen Farrell.

ALI MACGRAW
appears in the film *Love Story*, 1970.

DAVID BYRNE
and Talking Heads appear in the film *Stop Making Sense*,
1984.

LIZZIE BORDEN,
accused of murdering her stepmother and father with an
ax, is acquitted, 1892.

SALVADOR DALI,
Spanish surrealist painter, arrives at the London Surrealist Exhibition of 1938—dressed in a deep-sea-diving
suit.

JUDY GARLAND
stars in the classic film *A Star Is Born*, 1954.

MARGARET SANGER,
American family planning pioneer, is arrested for distributing birth control information, deemed "obscene" by the authorities, New York, 1915.

HENRY DAVID THOREAU,
arrested for refusing to pay taxes to support the Mexican War of 1846, writes "Civil Disobedience," 1849. This essay was used as a manual by Gandhi and Dr. Martin Luther King, Jr.

NIKOLA TESLA,
a Croatian, patents the alternating current electric motor, which he sells to George Westinghouse, 1888.

GEORGE LUCAS
directs the film *Star Wars*, 1977.

CECIL B. DEMILLE,
the son of an Episcopal priest, forms a partnership with Jesse Lasky to produce DeMille's first movie, *The Squaw Man*, 1914.

BERNARDO BERTOLUCCI,
Italian film director, makes the controversial X-rated film *Last Tango in Paris*, starring Marlon Brando, 1971.

GORDON COOPER
is the youngest of the men selected to be Project Mercury astronauts, 1959.

GEORGE HERMAN "BABE" RUTH
sets the record of sixty home runs in a single season, 1927.

JAMES ARNESS
makes his debut as Marshal Matt Dillon in the television series "Gunsmoke," 1955.

ROD CAREW
is the American League Batting Champion for the sixth
time, 1977, with an average of .388.

age thirty-three

JESUS CHRIST
is crucified and resurrected, c. A.D. 29.

CHARLES LUTWIDGE DODGSON,
using the pseudonym Lewis Carroll, writes *Alice in Wonderland*, 1865.

FIDEL CASTRO
becomes prime minister of Cuba, 1959.

THOR HEYERDAHL
of Norway sets out from Peru for Polynesia in order to demonstrate that there was contact between the two cultures in ancient times, 1947. His voyage was recounted in the book *Kon Tiki*.

D. W. GRIFFITH
directs his first film, *The Adventures of Dollie*, 1908.

CHARLES GOODYEAR,
the future inventor of vulcanized rubber, is jailed for debt, 1834.

CHARLTON HESTON
appears as Moses in the film *The Ten Commandments*, the second version (the first being silent) produced by Cecil B. DeMille, 1956.

MARTIN LUTHER,
only two weeks before his thirty-fourth birthday, posts the ninety-five theses on the door of the church in Wittenberg, Germany, October 31, 1517. This is considered by many to be the crucial moment in the Protestant Reformation.

RICHARD NIXON
is elected to Congress, 1946.

MICHELANGELO
begins painting the Sistine Chapel, 1508.

DR. SEUSS
(Theodore Seuss Geisel) finally publishes his first book, *To Think That I Saw It on Mulberry Street*, which had been rejected by twenty-three publishers, 1937.

WYATT EARP,
marshal of Tombstone, Arizona, shoots Pat Garrett in the legendary gunfight at the O.K. Corral, 1881.

JEAN-PAUL SARTRE,
French existentialist philosopher, writes *Nausea*, 1938. Sartre was a first cousin of Albert Schweitzer.

CATHERINE THE GREAT,
a German princess, becomes empress of Russia, 1762.

ROBERT FULTON,
an American inventor, develops and successfully demonstrates a working submarine to the French, 1789. However, they were not impressed, and it would be a century before serious naval application of submarines would take place.

FRANCIS FORD COPPOLA
directs *The Godfather*, which won the 1972 Best Picture
Academy Award.

ANDRE MALRAUX,
French novelist, publishes *Man's Fate*, 1934. The book
was an account of the Chinese Revolution of 1928.

MARCEL DUCHAMP,
influential French painter of *Nude Descending a Staircase*, temporarily gives up art to pursue chess, 1920.

PRINCE RAINIER III
of Monaco marries American actress Grace Kelly, 1956.

CLAES OLDENBURG,
Swedish-born American sculptor, creates the ''soft''
sculpture *Dual Hamburger*, 1962. Oldenburg sculpts ev-
eryday objects, such as hamburgers, and once had a
''store'' that sold sculptures of food and household products.

THOMAS JEFFERSON
drafts the Declaration of Independence, 1776.

OMAR SHARIF
plays the title role in *Doctor Zhivago*, 1965.

ROD CAREW
is the American League Batting Champion for the seventh time, with an average of .333.

MARIE CURIE,
Polish-born French scientist, with her husband Pierre,
wins the Nobel Prize for their studies of radioactivity. Thus
she is the first woman to win a Nobel Prize, 1903.

MARY WOLLSTONECRAFT
of England publishes one of the earliest expressions of feminism, *A Vindication of the Rights of Women*, 1792. Her daughter, Mary Wollstonecraft Shelley, was the author of *Frankenstein*.

MARY TYLER MOORE
stars in the long-running television series "The Mary Tyler Moore Show," 1971.

BENJAMIN DISRAELI
is the first person born a Jew to serve in the British House of Commons, 1837.

GIOVANNI PAOLO LOMMAZO,
a painter of Milan, goes blind, 1571, and begins dictating books on art theory, for which he is now known.

EDGAR BERGEN,
father of popular actress Candice Bergen, goes on radio with his ventriloquism partner, Charlie McCarthy, 1936.

HENRY FORD
builds his first automobile, 1896.

MERYL STREEP
wins the 1982 Academy Award for Best Actress for *Sophie's Choice*.

WHITEY FORD,
pitcher for the New York Yankees, wins a record of ten World Series games. He wins the 1961 Cy Young Award.

WALTER DE MARIA,
American artist, creates his *Mile Long Drawing*, 1968. The work consisted of two-mile-long chalk lines spaced twelve feet apart in the Mojave Desert.

In World Heavyweight Boxing:
    JESS WILLARD defeats Jack Johnson in a twenty-sixth
    round knockout in Havana, Cuba, 1915; and
    JAMES SMITH defeats Tim Witherspoon in a first-
    round knockout, 1986.

FRANK LLOYD WRIGHT,
probably the most influential twentieth-century American
architect, builds the then-revolutionary Ward Willits
house in Illinois, 1902.

HARMON KILLEBREW
of the Minnesota Twins is the 1969 home-run (forty-nine)
and runs-batted-in (140) leader. He was also home-run
leader in 1962, 1964, and 1965. He was the RBI leader
in 1962 and 1971.

EVA PERON,
wife of Argentine dictator Juan Peron and the most powerful woman in the country, worshiped by millions, dies,
1952.

JOHN BELUSHI,
a comedian best known for his appearances on the television series "Saturday Night Live," dies of a drug overdose, 1982.

COUNT BASIE,
one of the greats of jazz, makes his debut at New York's
Roseland Ballroom, 1937.

IGNATIUS LOYOLA,
a former soldier and future founder of the Jesuit order,
is ordained a priest, 1526. Loyola recognized his calling
after the horrors of war and in thanksgiving for the heal-
ing of a serious war wound.

JOHN DEERE
invents the steel plow, 1837, capable of turning the heavy
sod of the American prairie.

age thirty-four

"My Lord Tomnoddy is thirty-four
  The Earl can last a few years more
My Lord in the Peers will take his place
Her majesty's councils his words will grace
  Offices he'll hold and patronage sway
  Fortunes and lives he will vote away
  And what are his qualifications? ONE
He is the Earl of Fitzdotterel's eldest son."
  —Robert Barnabas Brough (1828–60)

"This day I am, by the grace of God, thirty-four
years old, in very good health and mind's content,
and in condition of estate much beyond whatever
my friends could expect of a child of theirs, this
day thirty-four years. The Lord's name be praised!
And may I be thankful for it."
  —Samuel Pepys (1633–1703)

J. F. BIERLEIN
writes the *Book of Ages*, 1991.

MARY MAPES DODGE
writes *Hans Brinker, or the Silver Skates*, 1865.

AMELIA EARHART
makes the first solo transatlantic airplane flight by a
woman, 1932.

NORMAN VINCENT PEALE,
author of *The Power of Positive Thinking*, becomes pastor of Marble Collegiate Church, New York, 1932.

DIONNE WARWICK
takes a leave from her successful singing career to pursue a master's degree in music, 1974.

EDVARD MUNCH,
Norwegian expressionist painter, paints *Jealousy*, a study of the emotion that contains a self-portrait, 1897.

AMADEO PETER GIANNINI
establishes the Bank of Italy, forerunner of the Bank of America, San Francisco, 1904.

JOHN AUDUBON,
later America's greatest wildlife painter, is jailed for debt and released on a plea of bankruptcy, 1819.

ADOLF HITLER
unsuccessfully attempts to overthrow the Bavarian government in the Beer Hall Putsch of 1923.

WILLIAM SIDNEY PORTER,
better known as O. Henry, is called back to Texas to stand trial for bank embezzlement. He flees to Honduras and is then arrested when he returns to Texas to visit his dying wife. He was sentenced to three years in prison, 1896.

ELIJAH MUHAMMAD
founds the Nation of Islam, 1931.

OLIVER HARDY
teams up with Stan Laurel, thirty-six, 1926.

ARTHUR MILLER,
American playwright, wins the 1949 Pulitzer Prize for the modern classic *Death of a Salesman*.

GEORGE PULLMAN
introduces the Pullman railroad sleeping car, 1865. It was first used on the funeral train of President Lincoln.

JANE FONDA
wins the Best Actress Academy Award for *Klute*, 1971.

OTTO VON BISMARCK
makes a speech in the Prussian Parliament that comes to the attention of King Frederick William of Prussia and establishes his long career as a force behind the Germany unity movement under the leadership of Prussia, 1849.

KARL BENZ
builds his first gasoline engine in Mannheim, Germany, 1878.

HERNANDO CORTES
invades Mexico and conquers the Aztec Empire, 1520.

LEE DE FOREST
patents the triode vacuum tube, facilitating the development of radio, 1909.

EMMA WILLARD
establishes the Troy Female Academy, the first U.S. women's college, 1821.

ELIZABETH TAYLOR
wins the 1966 Best Actress Academy Award for *Who's Afraid of Virginia Woolf?*

PHIL COLLINS
wins the 1985 Best Album Grammy Award for *No Jacket Required*.

SIR EDMUND HILLARY
of New Zealand climbs Mount Everest, 1953.

HUGH LOFTING
writes the children's classic *Dr. Doolittle*, 1920.

THOMAS HARDY
writes *Far from the Madding Crowd*, 1874.

CHARLIE "BIRD" PARKER,
legendary jazz saxophone great, dies, 1955.

RAY CHARLES
is busted for possession of marijuana, 1964.

CLAUDE MONET
paints *Impression: Rising Sun*, giving rise to the term
"impressionism" to describe a style of painting, 1874.

RICHARD STRAUSS
composes *Ein Heidenleben* ("A Hero's Life"), a musical
treatment of his daily life, complete with the sound of a
baby crying, 1898.

ABDUL GAMAL NASSER,
with General Naguib, leads a military coup that over-
throws King Farouk of Egypt, 1952.

FLORENCE NIGHTINGALE
establishes battlefield hospitals for British soldiers in the
Crimean War, 1854.

MAXIM GORKY
writes *Lower Depths*, 1902.

CLINT EASTWOOD
appears in the first of the Sergio Leone "spaghetti" west-
erns, *A Fistful of Dollars*, 1964.

GARSON KANIN
writes the hit play of 1946 *Born Yesterday*.

RALPH WALDO EMERSON
writes his famous poem "Concord Hymn," 1837.

DOROTHY PARKER,
celebrated American wit, publishes her first book of
verse, *Enough Rope*, 1927.

BENJAMIN WEST,
an American by birth, is appointed court historian to King
George III of Great Britain, only four years before American independence, 1772.

WILLIAM FRIEDKIN
directs the film *The Exorcist*, the thriller film of demonic
possession, 1973.

GUSTAVE DORE
makes his famous illustration series for the Bible, 1866.

MAHALIA JACKSON
begins recording gospel music, 1945.

RUDOLF DIESEL
builds the first of the engines now known by his name,
1892.

BOB FITZSIMMONS
knocks out James Corbett in fourteen rounds to win the
World Heavyweight Boxing Title, 1897.

ANDY WARHOL
becomes famous as a leader of American "pop" art with
his *Campbell Soup Cans*, 1962.

MAE WEST
makes quite a name for herself by writing, producing,
directing, and acting in a play entitled *Sex*, 1926. The
play would have been R-rated in the 1990s. She was
charged with obscenity and spent ten days in jail.

age thirty-five

"Ladies, stock and tend your hive
Trifle not at thirty-five
For howe'er we boast and strive
Life declines from thirty-five."
　　　　　Samuel Johnson (1709–84)

(NOTE: The author bears no responsibility for the sexism inherent in any quotation.—J.F.B.)

"Women are most fascinating between the ages of thirty-five and forty after they have won a few races and know how to pace themselves. Since few women ever pass forty, maximum fascination can continue indefinitely."
　　　　　　　　　　　　　—Christian Dior

"I could not say I believe. I know! I have had the experience of being gripped by something that is stronger than myself, something that people call God. . . . Our heart glows and secret unrest gnaws at the roots of our being. . . . Dealing with the unconscious has become a question of life for us. . . . I have treated many hundreds of patients. . . . Among [those] in the second half of life—that is to say, over thirty-five—there has not been one whose problem in the last resort was not that of finding a religious outlook on life."
　　　　　　　　　　　　　—Carl G. Jung

HARVEY FIRESTONE
produces his first rubber tires at Akron, Ohio, 1903.

90

RENE LAENNAC
of France invents the stethoscope, 1819.

MARTIN LUTHER KING, JR.,
wins the 1964 Nobel Peace Prize.

MARILYN MONROE
makes her last film, *The Misfits*, 1961.

JACK BENNY
first appears on film, 1929.

DMITRI MENDELEEV
of Russia devises the periodic table of elements, 1868–69.

WOLFGANG AMADEUS MOZART
dies, 1791, after squandering a fortune and living in a paranoid state of fear that he was being poisoned.

WASHINGTON IRVING,
later the author of "Rip Van Winkle" and other popular works, takes up writing to support himself after the family hardware store fails, 1818.

SINCLAIR LEWIS,
after failing at a number of ventures, becomes recognized as a serious author with the publication of *Main Street*, 1920.

WILLIAM HURT
wins the 1985 Best Actor Academy Award for *Kiss of the Spider Woman*.

LOU BROCK
sets a baseball record by stealing 118 bases in the 1974 season.

JESSE JAMES
is fatally shot in the back, allegedly by Robert Ford, while straightening a picture on the wall of his home, 1882.

JAMES WHISTLER,
an American painter best known for his portrait of his mother, declares bankruptcy, 1879.

PETER BLAKE,
a leading British "pop" artist, produces his best-known work—the album cover of the Beatles' *Sergeant Pepper's Lonely Hearts Club Band*, 1967.

THADDEUS FAIRBANKS
invents the platform scale, 1831.

WILLIAM SHATNER
(Captain James Tiberius Kirk) and LEONARD NIMOY (Spock) make their debut in the television series "Star Trek," 1966.

KARL PEARSON
writes *The Grammar of Science*, a pioneer work in scientific use of statistics, 1892.

RAY BOLGER
appears as the scarecrow in *The Wizard of Oz*, 1939.

FRANCIS SCOTT KEY
writes "The Star-Spangled Banner," 1814.

PAUL CEZANNE
meets the great painter Manet and refuses to shake his hand, claiming that it has been days since the former washed, maybe even weeks, 1874.

FREDRIC MARCH
wins the 1932 Best Actor Academy Award for *Dr. Jekyll and Mr. Hyde*.

LOUIS SULLIVAN,
one of the greatest American architects, forms the firm of Adler and Sullivan, 1891.

JEAN TINGUELY,
Swiss-born artist, creates his *Homage to New York*, 1960. The work was designed to self-destruct, but the mechanism failed and caused a fire at the Museum of Modern Art.

LENA HORNE
finds herself the victim of a 1950s Hollywood blacklisting as a result of her close association with singer Paul Robeson, an American Communist, c. 1952.

ROBERT KOCH,
German physician, publishes his thesis on the bacterial causes of infection, 1878.

HARRY S TRUMAN,
future president of the United States and a recently discharged World War I veteran, opens a men's clothing store, 1919.

ROBERT BOYLE
of Ireland discovers that the pressure of a gas varies inversely with its volume, given constant temperature, 1662. This is now called Boyle's law.

WILLIAM RANDOLPH HEARST
publishes a series of sensational articles on alleged Spanish atrocities in Cuba that largely lead to the Spanish-American War of 1898.

JOHN STEINBECK,
who had written five novels, publishes his first best-seller, *Of Mice and Men*, 1937.

ROBERT ALTMAN
directs the film *M*A*S*H*, 1971.

LORETTA SWIT
debuts as "Hotlips" Houlihan in the television series, "M*A*S*H," 1972.

NIKOLAI GOGOL
of Russia writes his classic *Dead Souls*, 1844.

FRANCIS FORD COPPOLA
has a very good year in 1974. Although close to bankruptcy only a few years earlier, he directs the critically acclaimed film *The Conversation*. He also wins the Academy Award for Best Picture, Best Director, and Best Screenplay for *The Godfather II*.

LITTLE RICHARD (PENNIMAN)
makes a comeback, 1970. It is said that he once asked Jimi Hendrix to take off a glittery shirt, saying, "I'm the only one who is supposed to be pretty here."

ALFRED DREYFUS,
a Jew and a captain in the French army, is arrested for allegedly spying for Germany, October 1894. This became an international cause célèbre as it appeared obvious that the anti-Semitism of fellow officers had led to the baseless charge. The author Emile Zola wrote *J'accuse* ("I Accuse") to protest and proclaim Dreyfus's innocence. An examination of documents later showed that Dreyfus was innocent.

ROY ACUFF,
scheduled to make his Grand Ol' Opry debut as a fiddler, sings instead, 1938.

MICHAEL CIMINO
wins the 1978 Oscar for Best Director for *The Deer Hunter*. The film also wins Best Picture, Best Supporting Actor (Christopher Walken), Editing, and Sound.

FRANK BORZAGE
wins the first (1927–28) Academy Award for Best Director for the film *Seventh Heaven*.

JOHN BARTLETT
publishes the first edition of *Bartlett's Familiar Quotations*, 1855.

ERROL GARNER,
composer of "Misty," records his celebrated album, *Concert by the Sea*, 1957.

GORDIE HOWE
of the Detroit Red Wings hockey club, wins his sixth Hart Trophy (most valuable player in professional hockey) and his sixth Ross Trophy (leading scorer), 1963. He won the Hart Trophy in 1952, 1953, 1957, 1958, 1959, and 1963. He won the Ross in 1951, 1952, 1953, 1954, 1957, and 1963. In twenty-six seasons of professional hockey, Howe played 1,767 games and retired with 801 goals, 1,049 assists, and 1,850 points.

HORATIO ALGER
publishes the first of his "rags to riches" stories, *Ragged Dick*, 1868.

MAXIMILIAN,
an Austrian prince ruling as the French puppet emperor of Mexico, is executed by his former subjects, 1867.

JOHN ALDEN,
husband of the former Priscilla Mullins and Assistant
Governor of Plymouth Colony (Massachusetts), is held
on a technical charge of murder after two colonists are
killed in a raid on the colony, 1634.

EMMANUEL GOTTLIEB LEUTZE
paints the well-known *Washington Crossing the Delaware*, 1851. The flag in the painting was not adopted until
years after the event took place.

GRIGORI RASPUTIN,
Russian mystic, convinces Czarina Alexandra that he can
cure her son of hemophilia, thus becoming a bizarre,
dangerous, and influential member of the Russian Imperial Court, 1905.

VINCENT VAN GOGH,
working in Arles, France, paints two hundred canvasses
in fifteen months, 1888.

age thirty-six

REMBRANDT VAN RIJN
paints *The Night Watch*, 1642.

VINCENT VAN GOGH
paints *Starry Night*, 1888.

YUL BRYNNER
debuts on stage in *The King and I*, 1951.

JOHN F. KENNEDY
marries twenty-four-year-old Jacqueline Bouvier, 1953.

WILLIAM JENNINGS BRYAN
is nominated for the U.S. presidency by the Democrats
after an inspiring speech against the gold monetary standard, 1896. He is the youngest person ever nominated for
the presidency by either of the two major U.S. political
parties.

WILBUR WRIGHT
and his brother Orville have the first successful airplane
flight at Kitty Hawk, North Carolina, 1903.

GUSTAVE FLAUBERT
writes the classic *Madame Bovary*, 1857.

JOHN MAYNARD KEYNES
writes *The Economic Consequences of the Peace*, 1919. This book is the basis of the ''Keynesian'' economic theories that proved influential throughout the 20th century.

ALAN ALDA
debuts as Hawkeye Pierce in the television series ''M*A*S*H,'' 1972.

SAM HOUSTON
resigns as governor of Tennessee after his wife leaves him. He then goes to Texas, 1829.

SIR ARTHUR SULLIVAN,
composer, and William S. Gilbert, 42, lyricist, write *H.M.S. Pinafore*, their first major success, 1878. Gilbert and Sullivan communicated largely by mail, as they personally disliked each other.

LILLIAN HELLMAN
wins the New York Drama Critics Circle Award for *Watch on the Rhine*, 1941.

CHARLES BAUDELAIRE,
influential French poet, publishes *Les Fleurs du mal* (''The Flowers of Evil''), 1857. The work is condemned by the courts as ''immoral'' and ''obscene.''

DR. SEUSS
(Theodore Seuss Geisel) writes *Horton Hatches a Who*, 1940.

WALTER GROPIUS
founds the Bauhaus school of architecture, Germany, 1919.

THE DUKE OF ABRUZZI
of Italy sets a pre-oxygen mountain-climbing record, nearly reaching the summit of Mount Godwin Austen, 1909.

JACQUES EDWIN BRANDENBERGER
of Switzerland invents cellophane, 1908.

ELIZABETH BLACKWELL,
the first female physician in America, along with her sister, Emily, founds the Women's Medical College, 1857.

HENRY MANCINI
wins an Academy Award for the song "Moon River," written for the 1960 film *Breakfast at Tiffany's*.

WALT DISNEY
produces his first feature-length animation film, *Snow White and the Seven Dwarfs*, 1938.

JOHANN SEBASTIAN BACH
composes the *Brandenburg Concertos*, 1721.

POMPEY
is elected consul of Rome, 70 B.C.

C. S. FORESTER
writes *The African Queen*, 1935, basis of the 1951 Academy Award–winning film starring Humphrey Bogart and Katharine Hepburn.

MARGARET MITCHELL
publishes *Gone with the Wind*, 1936.

EDGAR ALLAN POE
publishes *Tales of Mystery and Imagination*, 1845.

HENRI DUNANT,
Swiss banker, founds the International Red Cross, 1864.

WILLIAM BURROUGHS
invents the adding machine, 1891.

PETE ROSE
of the Cincinnati Reds has the longest hitting streak in
baseball history, from June 14 to July 31, 1978.

MUHAMMAD ALI HAJ
defends his World Heavyweight Boxing Title against Leon
Spinks in fifteen rounds, September 1978. Earlier that
year, Spinks had defeated Ali, but the champ retired with
his title intact.

WALT WHITMAN
publishes *Leaves of Grass*, 1855.

CHARLTON HESTON
wins the 1959 Academy Award for Best Actor for *Ben
Hur*.

DICK VAN DYKE
makes his television series debut in, "The Dick Van Dyke
Show," 1961.

CHARLES MANSON
and his "family" of three followers are found guilty of
seven murders, 1971.

SIDNEY POITIER
wins the 1962 Best Actor Academy Award for *Lilies of
the Field*.

GEORGE OGLETHORPE
establishes the American colony of Georgia, 1732.

JOHN LUTHER "CASEY" JONES
applies the brakes to his train in order to save the lives of his passengers and crew, losing his own life in the process, 1900.

ADOLF HITLER,
in prison for attempting to overthrow the Bavarian government, writes *Mein Kampf ("My Struggle")*, the blueprint for Nazi Germany, *1925*.

CHARLES CHAPLIN
stars in the classic silent film *The Gold Rush*, 1925.

JOHNNY CARSON
debuts as host of NBC television's "Tonight Show," 1962.

W. C. FIELDS
is a famous vaudeville juggler in the Ziegfeld Follies, 1915.

GENE HACKMAN
is nominated for an Academy Award for Best Supporting Actor for *Bonnie and Clyde*, 1967—only six years after the beginning of his acting career.

GRETA GARBO
retires from acting, 1941.

JOE WALCOTT
defeats Ezzard Charles for the World Heavyweight Boxing Title, 1951.

ARTHUR FIEDLER
begins conducting the Boston Pops, 1930.

JOHN MILLINGTON SYNGE
writes *The Playboy of the Western World*, 1906.

WILLIAM MAKEPEACE THACKERAY
writes *Vanity Fair*, 1847.

GEORGE CLINTON
(The Parliaments), the king of "funk" music, makes the
P-Funk Earth Tour, a high point of the funk movement
in popular music, 1976.

FRANCIS BACON,
now acclaimed as Britain's greatest living artist, makes
the controversial *Three Studies for Figures at the Base of
a Crucifixion*, 1945.

age thirty-seven

M. SCOTT CARPENTER
is the second American to orbit the earth, 1962.

VLADIMIR I. LENIN
is forced to flee Russia, 1907.

HARRY S TRUMAN,
future president of the United States, closes the doors of
his men's clothing store as the business fails, 1921. Although he is advised to declare bankruptcy, he refuses to
do so. It took him nearly fifteen years to repay the ten
thousand dollars in debts.

PETER ILYICH TCHAIKOVSKY
composes the ballet *Swan Lake*, 1877.

MARGARET HAMILTON,
a former kindergarten teacher, plays the role of the
Wicked Witch of the West in the film *The Wizard of Oz*,
1939.

TENNESSEE WILLIAMS
writes the classic play *A Streetcar Named Desire*, 1948.

ROBERT BURNS,
Scottish poet, dies, 1796.

JOHN GLENN
is the eldest of the Project Mercury astronauts, 1959.

CARY GRANT
appears in the film *The Philadelphia Story*, 1940.

JIM BOWIE
is killed in the Battle of the Alamo, 1836.

ANTHONY QUINN
wins the 1952 Best Supporting Actor Academy Award for *Viva Zapata*.

JAY LENO
is named "Permanent Guest Host" of television's "The Tonight Show," 1987.

STEVEN M. BABCOCK
invents a test to determine the butterfat content of milk, 1890.

WILLIAM PENN,
founder of Pennsylvania, makes his first visit there, 1682.

EMIL KOCHER
of Switzerland performs the first successful surgery to remove a goiter, 1878.

RICHARD BURTON
marries Elizabeth Taylor the first time, 1963.

SERGEI DIAGHILEV
establishes Les Ballet Russes, Paris, 1909.

HANS KREBS
discovers the Krebs cycle, explaining how tissues use carbohydrates in metabolism, 1937.

SEAN CONNERY
appears as James Bond in the film *You Only Live Twice*,
1967.

KARL MALDEN
wins the 1951 Academy Award for Best Supporting Actor
for *A Streetcar Named Desire*.

GAETANO DONIZETTI
writes the classic opera *Lucia di Lammermoor*, based on
Sir Walter Scott's *The Bride of Lammermoor*, 1834.

JOHN DALTON
of England proposes the atomic theory of matter, 1803.

FRANK CAPRA
wins the 1934 Best Director Academy Award for *It Happened One Night*.

LOUIS BLERIOT,
French aviator, is the first person to cross the English
Channel in an airplane, 1909.

FRANK SINATRA's
career seems over after he suffers a hemorrhage of the
vocal cords and is dropped by his talent agency, MCA,
1953. However, he made a dramatic recovery and won
the Best Supporting Actor Academy Award for *From Here
to Eternity*. He was paid only eight thousand dollars for
appearing in the film. He is still singing in 1991 and won
the 1965 Best Album Grammy Award and both the Best
Album and Best Record Grammy Awards for 1966.

ENRICO FERMI
wins the Nobel Prize in physics, 1938.

PATRICIA NEAL
wins the 1963 Best Actress Academy Award for *Hud*.

CARL JUNG,
hitherto considered the heir apparent of the psychoanalytic movement, breaks with his mentor, Sigmund Freud, fifty-six, 1912.

RONALD REAGAN
is divorced by Jane Wyman, 1948.

CISSY SPACEK
wins the 1980 Best Actress Academy Award for *Coal Miner's Daughter*, a film biography of country-and-western star Loretta Lynn.

ART CARNEY
debuts as Ed Norton in the television series "The Honeymooners," 1955.

GIOACCHINO ROSSINI,
Italian composer, writes the *William Tell* overture introducing his last opera *Guillaume Tell*, 1829. This piece is best known as the theme for the "Lone Ranger" radio and television series. Later the same year, Rossini takes a sabbatical from composing to study cooking.

GEORGES BIZET
composes his best-known work, the opera *Carmen*, and dies shortly thereafter, 1875.

GEORGE ARMSTRONG CUSTER
is killed in the Battle of the Little Big Horn, 1876.

HERMAN WOUK
wins the 1952 Pultizer Prize in fiction for *The Caine Mutiny*.

SAM GOLDWYN
produces his first motion picture, *Jubilo*, 1919.

CLARENCE DARROW,
who never finished law school, becomes the nation's most
famous lawyer after he defends Socialist leader Eugene V.
Debs in a labor strike case, 1894.

ULYSSES S. GRANT,
just two years before the Civil War and ten years before
he is inaugurated as president of the United States, is
fired from two jobs in one year, 1859. He was fired by a
real-estate office for his inability to collect rent pay-
ments, and then lost a job with the U.S. Customs House
in St. Louis.

THEODOR HERZL
presides over the first Zionist Congress, 1897, which
sought to establish an independent Jewish state. In addition to the biblical land of Israel in Palestine, delegates
considered Uganda as a possible site.

BOB HOPE
stars with Bing Crosby in the film *The Road to Singa-
pore*, 1940. The film also featured Dorothy Lamour clad
in a sexy sarong.

JULES VERNE
publishes his first book, *From the Earth to the Moon*,
1865. In this book he predicted many of the actual details
of the 1969 U.S. moon flight, including the rivalry between Texas and Florida for center of the U.S. space
effort.

MICHAEL LANDON
debuts as the father Charles Ingalls in the television series "Little House on the Prairie," 1974.

age thirty-eight

MARTIN LUTHER,
German religious reformer, practices what he preaches and marries an ex-nun, Katherina von Bora, 1521.

IRENE JOLIOT CURIE,
daughter of the 1903 Nobel Prize winners, Pierre and Marie Curie, shares the 1935 Nobel Prize in chemistry with her husband, Frederic. The Joliot Curies were later controversial for their Communist sympathies. Like her mother, Irene dies of radiation sickness contracted through her research.

GENERAL ANTONIO LOPEZ DE SANTA ANNA,
later the victor of the Battle of the Alamo, becomes president of Mexico, 1833. His life was full of strange ironies. For instance, although he is known as a Mexican military hero, he began his career as an officer in the Spanish army fighting *against* Mexican independence. Likewise, although he was the victor in the Battle of the Alamo, he went to Washington on behalf of Texas to lobby for annexation of Texas to the United States. He declared himself president of Mexico three times and was overthrown each time.

CLARK GABLE
plays Rhett Butler in *Gone With the Wind*, 1939.

T. E. LAWRENCE
writes *The Seven Pillars of Wisdom*, 1926, a record of his military exploits in the Arab war against the Turks during World War I. This book was the basis of the 1962 David Lean film, *Lawrence of Arabia*.

PEARL S. BUCK
writes her first book, *East Wind, West Wind*, 1930. Like her better-known work, *The Good Earth*, this book was set in China, where she grew up, the daughter of missionaries.

PAUL REVERE,
American master silversmith, best known for his ride of 1775, participates in the Boston Tea Party, 1773.

NEIL ARMSTRONG,
nearly thirty-nine, is the first human being to set foot on the moon, 1969.

JACK NICHOLSON
wins the 1975 Best Actor Academy Award for *One Flew Over the Cuckoo's Nest*.

VIVIEN LEIGH
wins her second Academy Award for Best Actress, this time for her performance as Blanche DuBois in *A Streetcar Named Desire*, 1951. Thus, although she was English, she won two Academy Awards for playing the Southerners, Blanche and Scarlett O'Hara.

ALEXANDRE DUMAS, SR.,
writes his first successful novel, *The Count of Monte Cristo*, 1840.

CHARLES GOODYEAR
recovers from bankruptcy to successfully vulcanize rubber, 1839.

BRODERICK CRAWFORD
wins the 1949 Best Actor Academy Award for *All the King's Men*, based on the book by Robert Penn Warren on the life of Louisiana governor and U.S. senator Huey P. Long.

CYRUS W. FIELD,
son of a Congregationalist minister, makes the first attempt to lay a telegraphic cable across the Atlantic, 1857. The cable broke 360 miles from shore.

FEDERICO GARCIA LORCA,
Spanish poet, is killed by Francisco Franco's fascist troops during the Civil War, 1936.

EDNA FERBER
wins the 1925 Pulitzer Prize in fiction for *So Big*.

WALT DISNEY
produces the film *Fantasia*, 1940.

ERNEST BORGNINE
wins the 1955 Best Actor Academy Award for *Marty*.

HANS CHRISTIAN OERSTED
of Denmark notices that the needle of a compass wavers when passed near an electric current—an important moment in the development of electromagnetic theory, 1819.

ALAN B. SHEPARD
is the first American to travel in outer space, May 5, 1961.

BING CROSBY
first sings ''White Christmas,'' written by Irving Berlin, in the film *Holiday Inn*, 1942.

JOSE FERRER
wins the 1950 Best Actor Academy Award for *Cyrano de Bergerac*.

ERNEST HEMINGWAY
writes *To Have and Have Not*, 1937.

THOMAS HARDY
publishes *Return of the Native*, 1878.

COUNT LEO TOLSTOY
writes *War and Peace*, 1866.

JANE AUSTEN
writes *Pride and Prejudice*, 1813.

GRANT WOOD
paints his most famous work, *American Gothic*, 1930.

PETER ILYICH TCHAIKOVSKY
composes the opera *Eugene Onegin*, 1878.

VASCO NÚÑEZ DE BALBOA
is the first European to see the Pacific Ocean from North America, 1513.

ROBERT H. GODDARD,
pioneer American rocket scientist, is ridiculed by *The New York Times* in 1920 for his prediction that rockets would someday carry men to the moon. The *Times* retracted its comments in 1969 following the Apollo moon flight.

QUEEN MARIE ANTOINETTE
of France is guillotined, 1792.

ARTE JOHNSON
joins the television series "Laugh-In," 1968.

HAROLD UREY,
American physicist, discovers heavy hydrogen, an important step toward the development of the atom bomb, 1931.

MARIO ANDRETTI
wins the 1978 Grand Prix.

LEON TROTSKY
becomes commissar of foreign relations in the new Soviet government, 1917.

RALPH WALDO EMERSON
publishes his *Essays*, including the famous "Self-Reliance," 1841.

JOHN LOGIE BAIRD,
a Scot, demonstrates the wireless transmission of pictures, which he names "television," 1926.

EDWIN LAND
produces the first "self-developing" camera, the "Polaroid," 1947.

SALLY FIELD
wins the 1984 Best Actress Academy Award for *Places in the Heart*.

ETHAN ALLEN,
Vermont patriot, and his "Green Mountain Boys" take Fort Ticonderoga from the British, 1778.

ADMIRAL RICHARD BYRD
flies over the South Pole, 1927.

BIG BILL HEYWOOD,
leader of the radical labor union the "Wobblies," or International Workers of the World, is acquitted of murdering the former governor of Idaho, 1907.

ALDOUS HUXLEY
writes *Brave New World*, 1932.

age thirty-nine

JACK BENNY
turns thirty-nine, 1933, and remains that age until his
death in 1974.

PETER COOPER
builds the *Tom Thumb*, the first steam locomotive to op-
erate commercially in the United States, 1830.

BENITO MUSSOLINI
becomes dictator of Italy, 1922.

HAILE SELASSIE
(born Ras Tafari) becomes emperor of Ethiopia, 1930.
The Rastafarian sect of Jamaica believes that Selassie is
an incarnation of God, and has never died.

GEORGE GERSHWIN,
American composer, dies, 1937.

WILLIAM RANDOLPH HEARST,
the nation's most influential newspaper publisher, is
elected to the United States Congress from New York,
1902.

PETER SELLERS
first appears as Inspector Clouseau in the films *The Pink
Panther* and *A Shot in the Dark*, 1964.

DINAH WASHINGTON,
legendary blues singer, dies, 1963.

PANCHO VILLA
crosses the border and raids Columbus, New Mexico, in
retaliation for the United States invasion of Mexico, 1916.

CHARLES GUITEAU,
a disgruntled federal job seeker, shoots President Garfield, 1881.

JACK PAAR
becomes host of television's "Tonight Show," 1957.

ULYSSES S. GRANT,
thrown out of the U.S. army for drunkenness, becomes
a general in the Union army, 1861.

RICHARD NIXON
is elected vice-president of the United States, 1952.

J. ROBERT OPPENHEIMER
moves to Los Alamos, New Mexico, to direct the Man-
hattan Project, which developed an atomic bomb, 1943.

INGMAR BERGMAN,
famed Swedish film director, makes two of his classics,
Wild Strawberries and *The Seventh Seal*, 1957.

CHARLES BRONSON
appears in the classic Western film *The Magnificent
Seven*, 1960, based on Akira Kurosawa's *The Seven Samurai*.

TOSHIRO MIFUNE,
called the "Japanese John Wayne," appears in *The Seven
Samurai*, 1959.

JOHN HANCOCK
signs the Declaration of Independence, 1776.

ROBERT FROST
publishes his first poetry, 1913.

CHARLES SCHWAB
becomes president of the newly organized United States
Steel, 1901, made up of Andrew Carnegie's steel holdings as well as other companies.

FRANK CAPRA
wins his second Best Director Academy Award, for *Mr.
Deeds Goes to Town*, 1936.

CARDINAL RICHELIEU,
in the service of King Louis XIII, becomes the de facto
ruler of France, 1624.

CYRUS FIELD
again fails in his attempt to lay a telegraphic cable across
the Atlantic Ocean, June 1858. In August of that year,
Field successfully laid a cable between Newfoundland
and Ireland. The cable's insulation failed, however, and
four weeks later it failed to function.

FRANKLIN DELANO ROOSEVELT,
future president of the United States, is stricken with
polio, 1921.

JEAN-PAUL SARTRE,
the voice of French existentialism, writes the classic play
No Exit, 1944.

ALICE WALKER
writes *The Color Purple*, winning the 1983 Pulitzer Prize
for fiction.

EDGAR RICE BURROUGHS
writes *Tarzan of the Apes*, 1914.

JACKIE GLEASON
debuts as Ralph Kramden in the television series "The Honeymooners," 1955.

LUDWIG VAN BEETHOVEN
composes one of the best known of his symphonies, No. 5 in C Minor, 1809.

JAMES STEWART
stars in the Christmas classic film *It's a Wonderful Life*, 1947.

GLENN T. SEABORG
of the United States wins the 1951 Nobel Prize in chemistry. Seaborg discovered five of the elements in the periodic table.

BEN KINGSLEY
wins the 1982 Best Actor Academy Award for *Gandhi*.

DOROTHEA EIXLEBEN
graduates from the University of Halle (Germany) and is the first female physician in Western Europe, 1754.

AMELIA EARHART,
American pioneer aviatrix, disappears, 1937.

MARTIN LUTHER
translates the Bible into German, 1522.

SIGMUND FREUD
collaborates with Josef Breuer on *Studies in Hysteria*, 1895.

EDWARD ALBEE,
American playwright, wins the 1967 Pulitzer Prize in drama for *A Delicate Balance*.

MAHALIA JACKSON
introduces gospel music to Carnegie Hall, 1950.

✓ ANTON VAN LEEUWENHOEK
of the Netherlands invents the microscope, 1671.

ROALD AMUNDSEN
of Norway is the first to reach the South Pole, 1911.

JOHN EDWARD PAYNE,
who wrote the words to ''Home Sweet Home,'' is jailed for debt, London, 1820. Ironically, he spent much of his own life homeless.

CLEOPATRA,
Queen of the Nile, commits suicide, 30 B.C. She had her brother executed to ensure that Caesarion, her son by Julius Caesar, would be the undisputed heir to the throne. Tradition says that she killed herself by taking an asp, or perhaps a horned viper, out of a basket of figs, placing it on her wrist, and being poisoned by its venom.

HERNANDO DE SOTO
discovers the Mississippi River, 1539.

FRANCIS ASBURY,
once accused of collaboration with the British during the American Revolutionary War, is chosen by John and Charles Wesley to direct the Methodist societies in North America. A tireless preacher, Asbury founded the Methodist Episcopal Church, forerunner of today's United Methodist Church, 1784.

SERGEI EISENSTEIN,
considered the greatest early Soviet filmmaker, is de-
nounced by *Pravda*, 1937.

TED WILLIAMS
of Boston is the American League Batting Champion for
the third time, 1957, with an average of .388.

ALFRED BINET
develops the IQ test, 1896.

age forty

"Fair and fat and forty was the toast of all the young men."
  —Irish playwright John O'Keefe (1747–1833),
  Irish Minnie

"At twenty years of age, the will reigns; at thirty, the wit; and at forty, the judgement."
  —Benjamin Franklin

"Every man over forty is a scoundrel."
  —George Bernard Shaw

"Fair, fat and forty."
  —Sir Walter Scott, *St. Ronan's Well*

"We don't understand life any more at forty than we did at twenty, but we know it and admit it."
  —Jules Renard

"Find a man of forty who heaves and moans over a woman in the manner of a poet and you will behold either a man who ceased to develop intellectually at twenty-four or thereabouts, or a fraud who has his eye on the lands, tenements, and hereditaments of the lady's deceased husband."
  —H. L. Mencken

"I am resolved to grow fat and look young till forty, and then to slip out of the world with the first wrinkle and the reputation of five and twenty."
  —John Dryden

"Forty—sombre anniversary to the hedonist—in seekers after truth like Buddha, Mahomet, Mencius, St. Ignatius, the turning point of their lives."

—Cyril Connolly, *The Unquiet Grave*

"When you're forty, half of you belongs to the past."

—Jean Anouilh

"Better one bite of forty's bitter rind than the hot wine that gushed forth from the vintage of twenty."

—James Russell Lowell

"From forty to fifty, a man is at heart either a stoic or a satyr."

—Sir Arthur Wing Pinero

"The best years are the forties; after fifty a man begins to deteriorate, but in the forties he is at the height of his villainy."

—H. L. Mencken

"It is in the thirties that we want friends. In the forties we know they won't save us any more than love did."

—F. Scott Fitzgerald

*"Ho pretty page with the dimpled chin
That never has known the barber's shear
All your wish is woman to win
This is the way that boys begin
Wait till you come to Forty-year.*

*Forty times over let Michaelmas pass
Grizzling hair the brain doth clear
Then you know a boy is an ass
Then you know the worth of a lass
Once you have come to Forty-year."*

—William M. Thackeray

> *"To hold the same views at forty as we do at twenty is to have been stupefied for a score of years and to take rank, not as a prophet, but as an unteachable brat, well birched and none the wiser."*
> —Robert Louis Stevenson

TED WILLIAMS
is again, the fourth time, the batting champion of the American League, with an average of .328.

MARK TWAIN
(born Samuel L. Clemens in October 1835), writes *Tom Sawyer*, 1876.

JOHN F. KENNEDY,
U.S. senator from Massachusetts, wins a 1957 Pulitzer Prize for *Profiles in Courage*.

RUDYARD KIPLING
publishes his first novel, *Kim*, 1905.

LECH WALESA,
a former shipyard electrician, wins the 1983 Nobel Peace Prize for his work as leader of Poland's independent trade union, Solidarity.

NATHAN BEDFORD FORREST
enlists in the Confederate army as a private early in 1861 and is a major general by October.

D. W. GRIFFITH
makes the silent film masterpiece *Birth of a Nation*, 1915.

JOHN GLENN
is the first American astronaut to orbit the earth, 1962.

JAMES JOYCE
publishes his first successful novel, *Ulysses*, 1922.

HENRY AARON
of the Atlanta Braves, in his twenty-first season in major league baseball, breaks Babe Ruth's career-home-run record of 714 by batting number 715 against the Los Angeles Dodgers in Atlanta, 1974. His career statistics are staggering; 755 home runs, 3,771 hits, and 2,174 runs scored.

DUBOSE HEYWARD
writes *Porgy*, a portrait of life among South Carolina blacks, 1925. It is the basis of Gershwin's *Porgy and Bess*.

LADY ASTOR
is the first woman ever elected to the British Parliament, 1919. What is more remarkable is that she was born an American, Nannie Langhorn, in Virginia.

JOHN LENNON
is fatally shot outside his apartment in the Dakota, New York, 1980.

PATRICK HENRY,
Virginia patriot leader and orator, is this age at the time of American independence, 1776.

JOHN ADAMS,
Massachusetts patriot leader and future president of the United States, is this age at the time of American independence, 1776.

NAPOLEON BONAPARTE,
having divorced Josephine, marries the teenage Maria Theresa of Austria in hopes of producing an heir, 1809.

GENE HACKMAN
wins the 1971 Best Actor Academy Award for *The French Connection*.

ZANE GREY
writes *The Lone Star Ranger*, prototype of the "Lone Ranger" radio and television series, 1915.

MICHAEL FARADAY
discovers the principles of electromagnetic induction, 1831.

SIR THOMAS LIPTON
goes into the tea business, 1890.

HENRY MANCINI
wins an Academy Award for the musical score of *The Pink Panther*, 1964.

MARCEL DUCHAMP,
celebrated French artist, marries, 1927. After a week of listening to his incessant lectures on chess, his bride glues the chessmen to the board and leaves him.

C. S. FORESTER
writes *Horatio Hornblower*, 1939.

GIUSEPPE VERDI,
Italian composer, writes the opera *Il Trovatore*, 1853.

LUDWIG VAN BEETHOVEN
composes his only opera, *Fidelio*, 1810.

CLARA BARTON,
future founder of the American Red Cross, sets up battlefield hospitals during the American Civil War, 1861.

GEORGE ORWELL
(pen name of Eric Blair) writes *Animal Farm*, 1943, a satirical look at the Soviet Union.

OLIVER STONE,
an American Vietnam veteran, wins the 1986 Best Director Academy Award for *Platoon*.

JOEL GREY
(born Joel Katz) wins the 1972 Best Supporting Actor Academy Award for *Cabaret*.

JON VOIGHT
wins the 1978 Best Actor Academy Award for *Coming Home*.

SIR ERNEST RUTHERFORD
works out the nuclear theory of the atom, 1911.

MILTON BERLE
becomes Mr. Television, the first bona fide national television star, through his "Texaco" show, 1948.

BARTOLOMEO CRISTIFORI
invents the piano, c. 1675.

DR. JONAS SALK
develops a polio vaccine and begins experimental vaccinations, 1954.

JAMES WATT's
steam engine, patented in 1769, is put to practical use, 1776.

EDWIN DRAKE
drills the world's first commercial oil well, Titusville, Pennsylvania, 1859.

MARY ANN EVANS,
writing under the name George Eliot, publishes the classic *Adam Bede*, 1859.

CAPTAIN JAMES COOK
leaves England on his first voyage to the South Seas, 1768.

JACOB COXEY
leads his "army" of unemployed from Ohio to Washington, 1894.

ANTHONY TROLLOPE,
hitherto of the British postal service, publishes the first of the Barsetshire novels for which he is famous, *The Warden*, 1855.

THOMAS PAINE,
author of the American Revolutionary tract *Common Sense*, is destitute and living off the charity of friends, 1777.

BING CROSBY
wins the 1944 Best Actor Academy Award for *Going My Way*. The film also won Best Picture and Best Director (Leo McCarey), and Barry Fitzgerald won Best Supporting Actor.

CHARLES GOUNOD,
French composer, writes his best-known opera, *Faust*, 1859.

age forty-one

CHRISTOPHER COLUMBUS
lands in the New World, 1492.

ELISHA GRAY
files a patent on the telephone only two hours after Alexander Graham Bell had registered his claim, 1876.

SIR LAURENCE OLIVIER
wins the 1948 Best Actor Academy Award for the film *Hamlet*.

YUL BRYNNER
wins the 1956 Best Actor Academy Award for *The King and I*.

HARRIET BEECHER STOWE
writes *Uncle Tom's Cabin*, 1852.

ELISHA GRAVES OTIS
invents the modern safety elevator, 1852.

JOAN CRAWFORD
wins the 1945 Best Actress Academy Award for *Mildred Pierce*.

JAMES A. MICHENER
wins a 1948 Pulitzer Prize for *Tales of the South Pacific*.

LUDWIG MIES VAN DER ROHE,
influential German, then American, architect, designs his
first building independently, 1927.

EDWARD EVERETT HALE
writes the classic "The Man Without a Country," 1863.

OSCAR WILDE
files a libel suit after having been accused of homosexual
relations with Alfred, Lord Douglas. When the truth of
the allegations emerges, Wilde is arrested while having
a drink with Lord Douglas in a hotel bar, and then jailed
for immorality, 1895.

PAUL REVERE
rides through the Massachusetts countryside to warn that
"the British are coming," 1775.

CHESTER A. ARTHUR
is appointed collector of the Port Authority of New York,
1871. Despite the resulting scandals over corruption and
patronage at the Port Authority, Arthur was personally
unscathed and was chosen as the Republican nominee for
vice-president in 1880. He succeeded to the presidency
upon the death of President Garfield in 1881.

DANIEL BOONE
establishes the settlement at Boonesboro, Kentucky,
1775.

KARL BENZ
builds his first automobile, the first gasoline-engine self-
propelled vehicle, 1885.

ARTHUR MILLER,
American playwright, is convicted of contempt of Congress
for refusing to give names of suspected Communists, 1956.
The conviction was later overturned.

W. H. AUDEN
wins the 1948 Pulitzer Prize in poetry for *The Age of Anxiety*.

ARTURO TOSCANINI
becomes principal conductor at the Metropolitan Opera, New York, 1908.

SIR ROBERT PEEL
organizes the London Police Force, 1829. They are still known as ''bobbies'' in his honor.

CHARLES SCHWAB,
formerly president of U.S. Steel, becomes president of Bethlehem Steel, 1903.

FRANK CAPRA
wins his third Academy Award for Best Director, 1938, for *You Can't Take It with You*.

RICHARD RODGERS
composes the music for *Oklahoma!*, 1943.

MARY CASSATT,
the first important female American painter, paints *Lady at the Tea Table*, 1885. Cassatt was a very brave woman. She went to Paris to study art over the objections of her socially prominent family and had difficulty being taken seriously, not because of the quality of her art, but because of her socialite background and sex. She remains an important American artist, even though much of her work was done in France.

JEAN DUBUFFET,
a wine trader, leaves his business to embark on a phenomenal second career as an artist, 1942.

VICTOR HERBERT
composes *Babes in Toyland*, 1900.

AL JOLSON
appears in the first commercial "talkie" motion picture, *The Jazz Singer*, 1927.

GARY COOPER
wins the 1942 Best Actor Academy Award for *Sergeant York*.

SAMUEL F. B. MORSE,
a penniless painter, develops an interest in the possibilities of telegraphy. He had hoped to finance his development of the telegraph by painting under commission for the U.S. Capitol. Morse spent the first half of his life as the object of both pity and ridicule. Destitute, he was given a room atop a newspaper building owned by his brothers, where he ate, slept, and worked on the telegraph.

CHER
wins the 1987 Best Actress Academy Award for *Moonstruck*.

ENRICO FERMI
directs the first atomic chain reaction, 1942.

GENERAL ANTONIO LOPEZ DE SANTA ANNA
defeats the Texans at the Battle of the Alamo, 1836.

ERNEST HEMINGWAY
writes *For Whom the Bell Tolls*, 1940.

RICHARD STRAUSS
composes the opera *Salome*, which scandalizes the 1905 audience with "The Dance of the Seven Veils."

THORNTON WILDER
writes *Our Town*, 1938.

CLINT EASTWOOD
stars in *Dirty Harry*, the first of a wave of vigilante films, 1971.

JANE FONDA
wins her second Best Actress Academy Award, 1978, for *Coming Home*.

LUDWIG VAN BEETHOVEN
composes Piano Concerto No. 5 in E-flat Major (*Emperor*) in honor of Napoleon Bonaparte, 1811.

W. C. HANDY
composes the "St. Louis Blues," 1914. This is considered an important beginning of recorded blues and jazz music, probably one of the greatest contributions of black America to the world.

ROBERT CLIVE
comes another step closer to British mastery of India as the Mogul ruler grants him full revenue power over the Bengal, making the British-born Clive the de facto ruler of India, 1765.

age forty-two

"A boy may still detest age
But as far as me I know
A man has reached his best age
At Forty-Two or so."
—R. C. Lehmann (1856–1929),
editor of the British humor magazine *Punch*

DAVID LIVINGSTONE,
Scottish medical missionary and explorer, discovers the
Victoria Falls of the Zambezi River, Africa, 1855.

JOHANN STRAUSS, JR.,
and his orchestra first perform his "Blue Danube," 1866.

CAMILLE SAINT-SAENS
composes the opera *Samson et Dalila*, 1877.

GEORGE SANTAYANA,
Spanish-American philosopher, writes the five-volume
classic *The Life of Reason*, 1905–06.

HENRY FIELDING
writes *Tom Jones*, one of the earliest novels in English,
1749.

SIR JAMES M. BARRIE
writes *The Little White Bird*, in which the character Peter
Pan appears for the first time, 1902.

BESSIE SMITH,
"Empress of the Blues," is killed in an automobile accident, 1937.

ROD STEIGER
wins the 1967 Best Actor Academy Award for *In the Heat of the Night*.

SATCHEL PAIGE
is a forty-two-year-old rookie in the major leagues, 1948. A veteran of the old Negro League, Paige joined the majors the year after professional baseball was integrated.

GIACOMO PUCCINI,
Italian composer, creates the classic *Tosca*, 1900.

ANNIE OAKLEY
retires from Buffalo Bill's Wild West Show, 1902.

IMOGENE COCA
joins the early television comedy classic "Your Show of Shows," 1950.

KEMAL ATTATURK
becomes president of Turkey, 1922. He purges the country of all vestiges of Ottoman rule, outlawing the wearing of the fez and issuing a decree that henceforth the Turkish language would be written in the Roman, rather than the Arabic, alphabet.

ROBERT PENN WARREN
wins a Pulitzer Prize for *All The King's Men*, 1942. The book is a fictionalized account of the career of Louisiana governor and U.S. senator Huey P. Long.

THEODORE ROOSEVELT
is the youngest man ever to serve as president of the United States. As vice-president, he succeeded to the presidency upon the death of President McKinley in September 1901, the month before his forty-third birthday.

RUDYARD KIPLING
is awarded the 1907 Nobel Prize in literature.

JULES VERNE
writes *20,000 Leagues Under the Sea*, 1870.

WOODY ALLEN
wins the 1977 Academy Award for Best Director for *Annie Hall*. The picture also was chosen as Best Picture, and Diane Keaton won the Best Actress Oscar for her performance in the film.

HUMPHREY BOGART
appears as Sam Spade in *The Maltese Falcon*, 1941.

JOSEPH MCCARTHY,
U.S. Senator from Wisconsin, makes the first notorious allegation of widespread Communist infiltration of the U.S. government, 1950.

MEL BROOKS
directs *The Producers*, 1968.

GEORGIA O'KEEFE,
American artist, moves with her husband, photographer Alfred Stieglitz, to Taos, New Mexico, 1929. Her work took on a southwestern flavor for which she is famous.

LOUIS PASTEUR
discovers the process now known as "pasteurization," 1864. He never received any royalties for this discovery, which he considered his gift to the world.

EDWARD VIII
of Great Britain abdicates the throne in order to marry divorced American socialite Wallis Warfield Simpson, 1937.

WILLIAM S. GILBERT
writes the lyrics for the operetta *H.M.S. Pinafore*, 1878, composed by Arthur Sullivan.

HENRI ROUSSEAU
first exhibits his paintings, 1886. A customs inspector by profession, Rousseau had no formal training as a painter, but was well received by the public and critics.

BORIS KARLOFF
(born William Henry Pratt) stars as the monster in *Frankenstein*, 1930.

WILLIAM LYON MACKENZIE
leads the Rebellion of 1837 in Upper Canada (now Ontario), an important milestone toward confederation in 1867.

FRED ROGERS,
a Presbyterian minister, comes to Public Television with "Mister Rogers' Neighborhood," 1970.

JOHANN SEBASTIAN BACH
writes *The St. Matthew Passion*, 1727.

THE COUNT DI CAVOUR,
nobleman, journalist, and architect of Italian unity, becomes prime minister of the Piedmont, 1852.

AUGUST WILSON
wins the 1987 Pulitzer Prize in drama and the 1986–87 New York Drama Critics Circle Award for *Fences*.

GIOVANNI SCHIAPARELLI
identifies "channels" (Italian: *canali*) on the surface of the planet Mars, making science fiction a growth industry, 1877.

IGNAZ SEMMELWEIS,
Hungarian physician, demonstrates that childbed fever is caused by unsanitary procedures on the part of doctors, 1860. The fever killed about one out of every eight new mothers. His colleagues, however, so ridiculed him that he became mentally ill. He was vindicated in the end by Dr. Joseph Lister's studies and advocacy of antiseptic surgical procedures. However, he never lived to see himself vindicated.

NOEL COWARD
writes the play *Blithe Spirit*, 1941.

NOLAN RYAN,
a free agent pitching for the Texas Rangers, pitched his five thousandth strikeout, August 1989 in Arlington, Texas. It was Ryan's twenty-third year in major league baseball.

THOMAS EAKINS,
one of the greatest nineteenth-century American painters, is forced to resign his teaching post at the Philadelphia Academy of Fine Art, 1886. The reason: he had allowed both male and female students to sketch from a completely nude male model.

AMBROISE PARÉ
becomes surgeon to Henry II of France, 1552. He was a pioneer in improving the status of surgeons. Trained as a barber, as were most surgeons of the day, Paré was one of the first humane and relatively professional surgeons. He ended the practice of treating battlefield wounds by pouring boiling oil into them, and began tying off blood vessels during amputations.

age forty-three

"She may well pass for forty-three—in the dusk, with a light behind her."

—William S. Gilbert

"To exclude from positions of trust and command all those below the age of forty-four would have kept Jefferson from writing the Declaration of Independence, Washington from commanding the Continental Army, Madison from fathering the Constitution, Hamilton from serving as Secretary of the Treasury, Clay from being elected Speaker of the House, and Columbus from discovering America."

—JOHN F. KENNEDY (age forty-three)
in response to a comment by former President
Truman about Kennedy's youth, 1960.

ADAM SMITH,
economic philosopher of capitalism, writes *The Wealth of Nations*, 1776.

JOHN F. KENNEDY
is elected president of the United States, 1960. Kennedy is the youngest elected president; Theodore Roosevelt, who succeeded as vice-president upon the death of President McKinley, is the youngest to ever serve as president.

HUMPHREY BOGART
appears in the film *Casablanca*, 1942.

D. H. LAWRENCE
writes *Lady Chatterly's Lover*, 1928.

JOHANNES BRAHMS
composes his first symphony, 1876.

CLAUDE DEBUSSY,
French composer, applies impressionism to music in *La Mer* ("The Sea"), 1905.

MILOS FORMAN
wins the Best Director Academy Award for *One Flew Over the Cuckoo's Nest*, 1975. The film also won Best Picture, Best Director, Best Screenplay, Best Actor, and Best Actress.

PIERRE GUSTAVE TOUTANT BEAUREGARD
directs the bombardment of Fort Sumter, South Carolina, the first Confederate action against the Union, 1861. The same year, he leads the victorious Southern forces in the First Battle of Bull Run.

EDWIN ARMSTRONG
develops FM (frequency modulation) radio in order to eliminate the problem of static, 1933.

WILLEM EINDHOVEN
of the Netherlands invents the electrocardiograph, 1902.

PETE ROSE
of the Cincinnati Reds baseball team retires, 1985. He holds an impressive range of baseball superlatives—most games played (3,562), most turns at bat (14,053), and most singles (3,125). He is the only player in the history of baseball to play more than five hundred games in five different positions, as well as the player with the most (twenty-four) years in the National League. He broke Ty Cobb's all-time batting record and retired with 4,256 hits.

WILLIAM STYRON
wins a Pulitzer Prize for *The Confessions of Nat Turner*, 1968.

KIRK DOUGLAS
stars in the movie *Spartacus*, 1960. He was also executive producer of the film.

MICHAEL DOUGLAS,
son of Kirk, wins the 1987 Best Actor Academy Award for *Wall Street*.

ROBERT REDFORD
wins the 1980 Best Director Academy Award for *Ordinary People*, which starred Redford and Mary Tyler Moore.

CHARLES TOWNES
leads the team that develops the laser, 1958.

JAMES CAGNEY
wins the 1942 Best Actor Academy Award for his portrayal of composer George M. Cohan in *Yankee Doodle Dandy*. Cohan, who always gave his birthday as July 4, was actually born on July 3.

ROSA BONHEUR,
painter of *The Horse Fair* and nineteenth-century France's most important female painter, is the first woman to be awarded the Gold Cross of the French Legion of Honor, 1865.

DIEGO RIVERA
paints probably his best-known work, *La Historia de México*, the mural at the National Palace, Mexico City, 1929.

CLARENCE BIRDSEYE
puts the first frozen food on the market—peas—in 1929.

JOSEPH CONRAD
writes *Lord Jim*, 1900. Born in Poland, Conrad is remarkable because he learned English as an adult and went on to be an important novelist in that language.

PAUL GAUGUIN,
tired of his wife and life as a Paris stockbroker, flees to Tahiti to paint, living with a fifteen-year-old native girl, 1891.

HIRAM MAXIM
invents his machine gun, 1883.

BORIS KARLOFF
stars in *The Mummy*, 1931.

MATTHEW HENSON,
a black American, places the U.S. flag on the North Pole as part of Robert Peary's 1909 expedition.

JOSEPH-MICHEL MONTGOLFIER
and his brother Etienne, thirty-eight, are the first humans to fly in a hot-air balloon. Among the onlookers at the flight was seventy-seven-year-old Benjamin Franklin, Paris, 1783.

JAMES MADISON,
future president of the United States, marries Quaker Dolley Payne Todd, twenty-six, 1794. Dolley is expelled from the Quakers for marrying outside her religion (Madison was an Episcopalian). She went on to become one of the most famous first ladies because of her skills as a hostess.

SIR ALEC GUINNESS
wins an Academy Award for Best Actor, for *Bridge on the River Kwai*, 1957.

CLIFF ROBERTSON
wins the 1968 Best Actor Academy Award for *Charly*.

SAMUEL ADAMS,
who had completely failed at every commercial endeavor, including running a brewery, turns to politics, 1764. A cousin of John Adams, he became an important patriot leader in the American Independence movement.

MANUEL DE FALLA,
Spanish composer, composes his best-known work, *The Three-Cornered Hat*, 1919.

KUBLAI KHAN
becomes Great Khan of the Mongols, 1259.

MARY LAMB,
a pioneer in children's literature, coauthors, with her brother, Charles ("Elia"), *Tales from Shakespeare* for young readers, 1801.

ULYSSES S. GRANT,
commander of the Union forces, accepts the surrender of General Robert E. Lee, commander of the Confederate Army of Northern Virginia, at Appomattox Court House, Virginia, 1865.

age forty-four

JOHN MILTON,
author of *Paradise Lost*, becomes completely blind, 1652.

ELIZABETH BARRETT BROWNING
publishes *Sonnets from the Portuguese*, 1850.

ROBERT WILHELM BUNSEN
of Germany invents the Bunsen burner, 1855.

SIR JAMES BARRIE's
Peter Pan is first performed on stage, 1904.

WARREN BEATTY
directs and stars in the film *Reds*, which is nominated for
Best Picture and wins him the 1981 Best Director Academy Award.

ALBERT CÁMUS,
French existentialist writer, wins the 1957 Nobel Prize
in literature. His thoughts on age: "Old age is passing
from passion to compassion."

SEAN O'CASEY,
Irish playwright, writes the classic *Juno and the Pay-
cock*, 1924. His thoughts on age are given under "Age
Eighty-one."

NICOLO MACHIAVELLI
writes the political-science classic arguing that ends justify means, *The Prince*, 1513.

PRINCE LOUIS-NAPOLEON,
nephew of Napoleon Bonaparte and the elected president of France, declares himself Emperor Napoleon III, 1852.

GEORGE ORWELL
(pen name of Eric Blair) retires to his farm in Scotland and writes the novel *1984*, 1947. It was published two years later.

MARIE CURIE
wins her second Nobel Prize, her first individually, in chemistry for her work with the elements radium and polonium, the latter named in honor of her homeland, Poland, 1911. Marie Curie died of radiation sickness contracted through her research.

AARON COPLAND
composes *Appalachian Spring*, one of his most popular works, 1944. This composition won him the 1945 Pulitzer Prize in music.

CAPTAIN JAMES COOK
of England is the first known man to cross the Antarctic Circle, 1772–73.

REVEREND JESSE JACKSON
seeks the Democratic nomination for president—the second time, 1988.

REVEREND ROBERT SCHULLER
begins the television broadcast of his "Hour of Power," 1970.

DR. CARL SAGAN,
Cornell University astronomer, wins a 1978 Pulitzer Prize
for *The Dragons of Eden*.

BETTE MIDLER
wins the 1989 Best Record Grammy Award for "Wind
Beneath My Wings."

INGRID BERGMAN
wins the 1956 Academy Award for Best Actress for *Anastasia*.

GENERAL WILLIAM TECUMSEH SHERMAN,
who had failed in virtually every civilian endeavor, leads
the destructive march through Georgia, 1864.

SADDAM HUSSEIN
becomes president of Iraq, 1979.

EDDIE FISHER,
American singer, declares bankruptcy, 1972.

GIACOMO PUCCINI
Italian composer, writes the opera *Madama Butterfly*,
1904.

MALCOLM X
is assasinated, 1965.

A. A. MILNE
writes *Winnie the Pooh*, 1926.

ADOLF HITLER
becomes chancellor of Germany, 1933.

FRANCISCO FRANCO
declares himself *caudillo*, fascist dictator of Spain, 1936.

SIGMUND FREUD
publishes the landmark *Interpretation of Dreams*, 1900.

JOHN FITCH
launches his first steamboat on the Delaware River, 1788.

BILLIE HOLIDAY,
blues legend, dies, 1959.

NIGEL BRUCE
appears as Dr. Watson in his first Sherlock Holmes movie
The Hound of the Baskervilles, 1939.

ANDREW YOUNG
is named U.S. Ambassador to the United Nations, the
first black American to hold this office, 1977.

TENNESSEE WILLIAMS
writes *Cat on a Hot Tin Roof*, 1955.

GRAHAM GREENE
writes *The Heart of the Matter*, 1948.

DR. CHRISTIAAN BARNAARD
of South Africa performs the first successful human heart
transplant, 1967.

JEAN HOUDON
sculpts his famous bust of George Washington, 1785.

ROBERT LOUIS STEVENSON,
Scottish author, dies after years of ill health, in Samoa,
1894.

SRIMAVO BANDARANAIKE
of Ceylon (now Sri Lanka) is the first elected woman
head of government in the world, 1960.

SIR FRANCIS BACON
advocates patronage of the sciences in *The Advancement of Learning*, 1605.

EDWARD TELLER
directs the development of the American hydrogen bomb, 1952.

FREDERICK SODDY
of Great Britain wins the 1921 Nobel Prize in physics. It is he who coined the word "isotope" to describe variations in atomic weight.

DICK HAYMES,
American popular singer, declares bankruptcy—the first time, 1960.

BERT LAHR
appears as the Cowardly Lion in *The Wizard of Oz*, 1939.

JOSEPH BEUYS,
German performance artist, performs *How to Explain Pictures to a Dead Hare*, Dusseldorf, 1965. The performance consisted of Beuys, his face covered with honey and gold leaf, carrying a dead hare through a gallery as he explained the pictures to it.

DICK MARTIN
stars in the television series "Rowan and Martin's Laugh-In," 1968.

LUTHER BURBANK
sells his plant nursery to devote himself to experimentation with the genetics of plants, 1894.

ANTON CHEKHOV,
Russian playwright and physician, dies of tuberculosis, 1904.

RICHARD HARRIS
stars in the film *A Man Called Horse*, 1976.

IVAN TURGENEV,
one of the greatest nineteenth-century Russian novelists,
writes the classic *Fathers and Sons*, 1862.

NELLIE TAYLOE ROSS,
Democrat of Wyoming, is the first woman elected governor of a U.S. state, 1924.

middle age

(NOTE: The first problem of middle age is defining it. Some sources start middle age at age thirty, most at forty, and some at forty-five. It generally ends about sixty, but given the youthfulness of our aging population, it might end at sixty-five or even seventy today. For the purposes of this book, we'll start it at forty-five and end it wherever the reader feels comfortable. I also ask your indulgence and tolerance of my following doggerel.)

> *My attention shifts from genitalia*
> *and all the desire of youth*
> *to hemorrhoids in full regalia*
> *falling hair and failing tooth.*
> *Never trust anyone over thirty*
> *in the sixties I was told*
> *but the thing that's really dirty—*
> *I have socks that are that old.*
> *My days of disco long are past:*
> *Middle age is closing fast!*
> —J. F. Bierlein (thirty-four)

"Men, like peaches and pears, grow sweet a little before they begin to decay."

—Oliver Wendell Holmes, Sr.,
The Autocrat of the Breakfast Table

"The years teach much which the days never know."
—Ralph Waldo Emerson

"Youth is wholly experimental."

> —Robert Louis Stevenson

"Boys are beyond the range of anyone's understanding, at least when they are between the ages of eighteen months and ninety years."

> —James Thurber

"Middle age is the time when a man is always thinking that in a week or two he will feel just as good as ever."

> —Don Marquis

> *"And youth is cruel, and has no remorse*
> *and smiles at situations it cannot see*
> *I smile of course*
> *and go on drinking tea."*
> —T. S. Eliot

> *"Of all the barbarous middle ages that*
> *which is most barbarous is the middle age*
> *of man; it is—I really scarce know what;*
> *But when we hover between fool and sage."*
> —Lord Byron, *Don Juan*

"I may not be Meethosalem, but I am not a child in arms."

> —Charles Dickens, *Dombey and Son*

> *"Sweet is the infant's waking smile*
> *And sweet the old man's rest*
> *But middle age by no fond wile,*
> *No soothing calm is blest."*
> —John Keble, "The Christian Year:
> St. Philip's and St. James' "

"Of middle age, the best that can be said is that a middle-aged person has likely learned how to have a little fun in spite of his troubles."

> —Don Marquis, *The Almost Perfect State*

"*To be interested in the changing seasons is, in this middling zone, a happier state of mind than to be hopelessly in love with spring.*"

—George Santayana, *Little Essays*

"*On his bold visage middle age
  Had slightly press'd its signet sage
  Yet had not quench'd the open truth
  And fiery vehemence of youth;
  Forward and frolic glee was there
  The will to do, the soul to dare.*"
—Sir Walter Scott, *The Lady of the Lake*

"*Let us, then love the perfect day,
  the twelve o'clock of life and stop
  The two hands pointing to the top,
  And hold them tightly while we may.*"
—Joaquin Miller, "The Sea of Fire"

"*Since more than half my hopes came true
  And more than half my fears
  Are but the pleasant laughing-stock
  Of these my middle years:—
  Shall I not bless the middle years?
  Not I for youth repine
  While warmly round me cluster lives
  More dear to me than mine?*"
—Sarah N. Cleghorn, "Contented at Forty"

"*Young in limbs; in judgement old.*"
—Shakespeare, *The Merchant of Venice*

"*Grow old along with me!
  The best is yet to be,
  The last of life for which the first was made;
  Our times are in His hand
  Who saith a first I planned
  Youth shows but half; trust God: see all
  Nor be afraid!*"
—Robert Browning, "Rabbi Ben Ezra"

"Your Lordship, though not clean past your youth, hath yet some of the smack of age in you, some relish of the saltness of time."

—Shakespeare, *Henry IV, Part Two*

"Middle age is a time of life
That a man first notices in his wife."
—Richard Armour

"Senescence begins and middle age the day
when your descendants outnumber your friends."
—Ogden Nash

age forty-five

"At eighteen, our convictions are hills from which we look, at forty-five they are caves in which we hide."
—F. Scott Fitzgerald, "Bernice Bobs Her Hair"

FYODOR DOSTOYEVSKY
publishes *Crime and Punishment*, 1866. Dostoyevsky knew his material well; he had been condemned to death. His sentence was later commuted to life, and he was finally pardoned.

FANNY FARMER
opens Miss Farmer's School of Cookery, Boston, 1902.

MOHANDAS GANDHI,
having worked for the civil rights of East Indians living in South Africa, returns to India, 1915.

BILL COSBY
stars in the television series "The Cosby Show," 1982.

OTTORINO RESPIGHI,
Italian composer, writes the orchestral suite *Pini di Roma* ("The Pines of Rome"), 1924.

E. M. FORSTER
writes *A Passage to India*, 1924.

BOB FOSSE
wins the 1972 Best Director Academy Award for *Cabaret*.

CHARLES NORDHOFF AND JAMES HALL,
both forty-five, write *Mutiny on the Bounty*, 1932.

PAUL SIMON
wins the 1987 Best Record Grammy Award for *Graceland*.

TINA TURNER
wins the 1984 Best Record Grammy Award for "What's Love Got to Do With It?"

SIR ROBERT WALPOLE,
the first prime minister of Great Britain, is jailed for corruption, 1711. Nevertheless, from 1721 to 1742, he was the most important man in Britain.

ALFRED, LORD TENNYSON
writes "The Charge of the Light Brigade," 1854, in honor of the battle of Balaklava in the Crimean War.

ALEXANDER POPE
writes his *Essay on Man*, 1733–34.

CLORIS LEACHMAN
wins the 1971 Best Supporting Actress Academy Award for *The Last Picture Show*.

JOHN CONSTABLE,
considered, with Turner, to be the greatest nineteenth-century British landscape painter, paints *The Hay Wain*, which wins him the Gold Medal at the Paris Salon of 1824.

JEAN DUBUFFET,
who had abandoned the wine trade to become a painter, has his first one-man exhibition, 1946.

J.R.R. TOLKIEN
writes *The Hobbit*, 1937.

P. T. BARNUM
declares bankruptcy, 1855. Some twenty years later, he would be fabulously successful with his first circus, The Greatest Show on Earth. In his own lifetime, he was as well known as a temperance lecturer as he was as a showman.

WERNHER VON BRAUN,
who had developed the German V-2 rocket in the 1930s, directs the launch of the first U.S. space satellite, Explorer, 1958.

LIONEL HAMPTON
is known as a jazz artist, but few people know of his influence in Republican politics. It is he who suggested the candidacy of Nelson Rockefeller for governor to the New York State Republican Committee. Rockefeller was elected governor in November that year, 1958.

JOSEPH CONRAD
writes *Heart of Darkness*, 1902. A reworking of the story set in wartime Vietnam is the basis of the 1979 film *Apocalypse Now*.

MARVIN GAYE,
American pop singer, dies, 1984.

DAN ROWAN
stars in the television series, "Rowan & Martin's Laugh-In," 1968.

age forty-six

"She's six and forty, and I wish nothing worse to happen to any woman."
                                        —Sir Arthur Wing Pinero,
                                        The Second Mrs. Tanqueray

RALPHE BUNCHE,
an American, is the first person of color to win a Nobel Prize, 1950. He won the Peace Prize in recognition of his efforts in the Middle East.

VICTOR HUGO,
French novelist, runs unsuccessfully for the French presidency, 1848.

SEAN O'CASEY,
Irish playwright, writes *The Plough and the Stars*, 1926.

RICHARD STRAUSS,
German composer, writes the opera *Der Rosenkavalier*, 1910.

THOMAS HARDY
writes *The Mayor of Casterbridge*, 1886.

BENJAMIN FRANKLIN
invents the lightning rod, 1752.

MARK TWAIN
writes *The Prince and the Pauper*, 1882.

ROALD AMUNDSEN
of Norway navigates the Northwest Passage from Greenland to Alaska, 1918–19.

SAMUEL JOHNSON
writes the first English dictionary, his *Dictionary of the English Language*, 1755.

WILL H. KELLOGG
organizes his cereal company at Battle Creek, Michigan, 1906.

LAJOS KOSSUTH
leads the unsuccessful Hungarian revolution of 1848.

WILLIAM VOGT,
a ''grandfather'' of the environmental movement, writes *The Road to Survival*, warning of the effects of chemicals and human intrusion on the life cycle of plants and animals, 1948.

EDGAR LEE MASTERS
writes *Spoon River Anthology*, 1915.

WALTER BRENNAN
is the first person to win three Academy Awards for Best Supporting Actor, 1940. Brennan won for *Come and Get It* (1936), *Kentucky* (1938), and *The Westerner* (1940).

CHUCK BERRY
has a number-one hit single ''My Ding-A-Ling,'' 1972.

CYRUS FIELD,
after three failed attempts to lay a transatlantic telegraphic cable, tries again. He nearly succeeds until the cable breaks just off the coast of Ireland, 1865.

M. C. ESCHER
of the Netherlands begins painting the optical illusions
for which he is famous, c. 1944.

LIEUTENANT COLONEL OLIVER NORTH,
formerly of President Reagan's National Security Council staff, is convicted as part of the Iran-Contra scandal.
Charges against North include obstruction of a congressional investigation and altering and destroying evidence,
1989.

LEO BAEKELAND,
a Belgian immigrant to the United States, invents "Bak-
elite," the first plastic, 1909.

FRANCISCO GOYA,
Spanish painter, loses his hearing and begins his most
productive period as an artist, 1792.

GUSTAV KLIMT
of Austria, is one of the great names in the art nouveau
style. He paints *The Kiss* in 1908, perhaps 1911.

ROBERT SCHUMANN,
German composer, insane as a result of syphilis, dies in
an asylum, 1856. He had committed himself after an unsuccessful suicide attempt.

CAROLUS LINNAEUS
of Sweden coins the words "genus" and "species" as
he begins the scientific classification of plants, 1753.

GREGORY PECK
wins the 1962 Best Actor Academy Award for *To Kill a
Mockingbird.*

HERMANN HESSE,
German novelist, writes *Siddhartha*, 1923.

WILLIAM RAMSAY
of Great Britain, who had already isolated the inert gases helium and argon, isolates krypton, neon, and xenon, 1898. He won a 1904 Nobel Prize for this work.

CARMEN MIRANDA,
Brazilian actress and singer, dies of a heart attack after a strenuous song-and-dance routine on the "Jimmy Durante" television show, 1955.

KING CAMP GILLETTE,
an American ("King" was his actual first name), patents the safety razor with disposable blades, 1901. He had invented it in 1896. While sales were slow at first, by 1904 it was a best-selling product.

FRANK CONRAD
of the Westinghouse Corporation begins the first regularly scheduled commercial radio broadcasts in America, from Pittsburgh's KDKA, 1920.

JOSEPH MCCARTHY,
U.S. senator from Wisconsin, is censured by the Senate after it is shown that his allegations of Communist infiltration of the U.S. government are baseless, 1954.

RICHARD GATLING
invents a machine gun that fires up to 600 rounds a minute; 1862. This is the source of the underworld slang use of "gat" for any automatic firearm, but especially a machine gun.

GALILEO
discovers the four bright moons of Jupiter, 1610.

NATHANIEL HAWTHORNE
writes *The Scarlet Letter*, 1842.

JEROME HOWARD,
born Jerome Horowitz, and better known as Curly of the Three Stooges, dies, 1952. He was the brother of Stooges Moe Howard (1897–1975) and Shemp Howard (1900–55). Curly had left the comedy team after suffering a stroke in 1946.

ALGER HISS,
U.S. State Department official, charged with being a Communist sympathizer, is found guilty of perjury and sentenced to prison, 1950.

SIGMUND FREUD
becomes professor of neuropathology at the University of Vienna, 1902.

FRANCIS CRICK
and James Watson, of Great Britain, accept a 1962 Nobel Prize for their discovery of DNA (dioxyribonucleic acid)—the basic "building block" of life.

ED SULLIVAN
becomes host of television's "Toast of the Town," later "The Ed Sullivan Show," 1948.

SAMUEL F. B. MORSE
demonstrates his invention, the telegraph, to a group of investors, 1837. They do not see the potential and are not interested.

LORD MOUNTBATTEN,
uncle of Prince Philip, the husband of Queen Elizabeth, becomes the last British Viceroy of India, 1946.

DEFOREST KELLEY
debuts as Dr. Leonard "Bones" McCoy on the television series "Star Trek," 1966.

PAUL CEZANNE,
French painter and a "bridge" between impressionism
and cubism, finally has his first one-man exhibition, 1895.

CARROLL O'CONNOR
makes his television series debut as Archie Bunker in
"All in the Family," January 1971.

EKATERINA FURTSEVA
is the first woman member of the Soviet Politburo, 1956.

age forty-seven

LEONARDO DA VINCI
paints *La gioconda*, popularly known as the *Mona Lisa*,
1499.

LORD NELSON
dies in a naval battle with the French at Trafalgar, off the
coast of Spain, 1805.

LYNDON BAINES JOHNSON,
future president of the United States, is the youngest man
to serve as majority leader of the United States Senate,
1955.

GEORGE S. KAUFMAN,
American critic and playwright, writes *You Can't Take It
with You*, 1936.

SIMÓN BOLÍVAR,
the "Liberator," who had led the nations of South America to independence from Spain, dies, 1830. He died a
disillusioned man after he was unable to maintain unity
among the South American nations.

CHARLES CHAPLIN
directs, appears in, and composes music for the film
Modern Times, 1936.

SIR ALEXANDER FLEMING
discovers penicillin, 1928.

WILLIAM C. DURANT
organizes General Motors, 1908.

PETE ROSE,
manager of the Cincinnati Reds, is suspended by the
baseball commissioner for gambling, 1989.

ROBERT BENTON
wins the 1979 Best Director Academy Award for *Kramer
vs. Kramer*.

WILLIAM WILBERFORCE
sees the culmination of his life's work as Great Britain
outlaws the slave trade, 1807.

ENRICO CARUSO,
Italian operatic tenor, makes his last stage appearance,
1920, in *La Juive* at the Metropolitan Opera, New York.

EDWARD ALBEE
wins the 1975 Pulitzer Prize in drama for *Seascape*.

VLADIMIR I. LENIN
becomes leader of the new Soviet government of Russia,
1917. (The name "Soviet Union" was not adopted until
1922.)

BERNARDO BERTOLUCCI
directs the film *The Last Emperor*, which wins the 1987
Academy Awards for Best Picture and Best Director.

RUDOLF HESS,
a leader of Nazi Germany, flies to England on a "peace"
mission and is interned for the duration of the war, 1941.

EDWARD JENNER
begins the practice of smallpox vaccination, 1796.

BASIL RATHBONE
first appears on film as Sherlock Holmes in *The Hound of the Baskervilles*, 1939.

LARRY HAGMAN
stars as J. R. Ewing in the television series "Dallas," 1978.

IDA TARBELL
becomes the first of the famous "muckrakers" of American journalism with her exposé *History of the Standard Oil Company*, 1907.

HERMAN MELVILLE,
author of *Moby Dick*, takes a job with the U.S. Customs Service to support his family, 1866.

PIET MONDRIAN,
Dutch painter, abandons impressionism and begins painting in straight lines and primary colors only, 1919.

JEAN STAPLETON
debuts as Edith Bunker in the television series "All in the Family," 1971.

HENRI DUNANT,
founder of the International Red Cross, declares bankruptcy, 1875.

SAMUEL F. B. MORSE
has a demonstration of the telegraph before the Congressional Appropriations Committee in hopes of obtaining funds for its development. They are not interested, 1838.

GUSTAV MAHLER
writes the masterpiece Symphony No. 8, 1907.

BURT LANCASTER
wins the 1960 Best Actor Academy Award for *Elmer Gantry*, based on the Sinclair Lewis novel of a corrupt evangelist.

GROVER CLEVELAND
is inaugurated to his first term as president of the United States, 1885. Cleveland is the only president to serve two nonconsecutive terms of office. His terms were separated by the term of President Benjamin Harrison. Cleveland, the son of a Presbyterian minister, is also the only president to be married in the White House. During Cleveland's 1884 campaign, it was revealed that he had fathered an illegitimate child. The Republican opposition responded by chanting "Ma, Ma, where's my pa?" Cleveland acknowledged the child and it quickly became a nonissue. Another interesting thing about Cleveland is that he underwent surgery to remove a cancerous part of his jaw while in office, a fact that remained secret until he was out of office.

MARLON BRANDO
appears in the controversial X-rated film *Last Tango in Paris*, directed by Bernardo Bertolucci, 1971. That same year he worked on *The Godfather*, for which he won a 1972 Academy Award for Best Actor, which he declined. *The Godfather* also won the Best Picture Academy Award and established the career of Francis Ford Coppola.

VITUS BERING,
a Dane in the service of Russia, proves that Siberia and North America are separated by a body of water, now known as the Bering Strait, 1727–29.

JOHN GORRIE,
a Florida physician, patents the first mechanical refrigeration device, 1851. Gorrie devised the system in order to keep his patients comfortable during hot weather. It would be a number of years before the commercial applications of refrigeration would be seen, and Gorrie never realized any significant financial gain as the result of his invention.

NICHOLAS LEBLANC
develops a process to separate soda from common salt, 1785.

CYRUS FIELD
finally succeeds in laying a transatlantic telegraphic cable, 1866.

LECH WALESA,
former shipyard electrician and leader of the Solidarity trade union, is elected president of Poland, 1990. It is the first free presidential election certainly since World War II, and arguably ever in Polish history. Free parliamentary elections had taken place in 1989 with Walesa's Solidarity slate winning a landslide.

DR. HUEY NEWTON,
founder of the Black Panthers, dies, 1988.

GEORGE OGLETHORPE,
founder of the colony of Georgia, is court-martialed and acquitted after failing to take the Spanish fort at St. Augustine (Florida), 1743. By this time, Oglethorpe was so deeply in debt and so disillusioned that he had to return to England.

NATHANIEL HAWTHORNE
writes *The House of the Seven Gables*, 1851.

GEORGE BERNARD SHAW

writes the play *Man and Superman*, 1903. Already a well-known critic, Shaw was the most popular playwright of his day.

age forty-eight

*"Not so young to love a woman for singing, nor
so old to dote on her for anything. I have on my
back forty-eight."*

—Shakespeare, *King Lear*

JOSEPH STALIN
expels his rival, Leon Trotsky, from the Soviet Communist party, thus becoming the undisputed ruler of the
Soviet Union, 1927.

JOHN DUNLOP
of Scotland patents the pneumatic tire, 1888. He developed the tire in order to give his son a smoother bicycle
ride to school. He sold the rights to his invention in 1894
and thus possibly missed out on a fortune once the tires
were adapted to automobiles.

WILLIAM JAMES,
American pioneer psychologist, who had himself suffered from debilitating depression, writes the landmark
Principles of Psychology, 1890.

VLADIMIR I. LENIN,
leader of the new Soviet state, is shot and wounded by a
political opponent, 1918. Although Lenin survived the
wound, it further weakened his constitution, which bore
the results of overwork, and he died at age fifty-four in
1924.

MEL BROOKS
directs the film *Young Frankenstein*, 1974.

MRS. OVETA CULP HOBBY

is appointed by President Eisenhower to serve as the first secretary of the newly created Department of Health, Education and Welfare, 1953. The department was reorganized in 1979 and is now represented by the Department of Education and the Department of Health and Human Services.

DALE CARNEGIE

writes the classic self-help book *How to Make Friends and Influence People*, 1936.

JOHN JACOB ASTOR,

successful fur trader and future supermillionaire, loses his profitable fur trading post at Astoria (Oregon), which is taken by the British during the War of 1812. Nevertheless, Astor prospered, dying with an estate totaling $20 million, 1848.

JACK LEMMON

wins the 1975 Best Actor Academy Award for *Save the Tiger*.

FRANZ ACHARD

builds the first factory to extract sugar from beets, Prussia, 1801. This has a dramatic impact on the world's economy, which had previously depended on sugarcane plantations in the West Indies and Louisiana.

BELA LUGOSI

stars in the film *Dracula*. When Lugosi died in 1956, he was buried in his alter ego's cape. Unlike either his character or Elvis, Lugosi hasn't been seen since.

HIRAM REVELS

of Mississippi is the first African-American to serve in the United States Senate, 1870.

SAM RAYBURN
of Texas becomes speaker of the House of Representatives, 1940. Rayburn served as speaker for seventeen years, beginning in 1940, interrupted by four years of Republican control, and ending with his death in 1961.

GUSTAV MAHLER
composes *The Song of the Earth*, 1908.

GERALDINE FERRARO,
nearly forty-nine, is the first woman nominee of a major American political party, 1984. She was nominated by the Democrats for vice-president as Walter Mondale's running mate.

GENERAL GEORGE MEADE
commands the victorious Union army at the Battle of Gettysburg—the largest land battle ever held on the North American continent, 1863. Lee's Confederates totaled 75,000 and suffered over 20,000 casualties. Meade's Yankees totaled 90,000 and suffered 18,000 casualties. The veterans of Gettysburg held their last encampment in 1938, the seventy-fifth anniversary of the battle.

STENDHAL,
a French novelist born Henri Beyle, writes the classic *The Red and the Black*, 1831.

EZRA CORNELL,
future founder of Cornell University and the largest single telegraph stockholder in America, organizes Western Union, 1855. Cornell had been the chief engineer working under Sam Morse at the successful 1844 demonstration of the telegraph.

OLIVER WENDELL HOLMES, SR.,
suggested the name *Atlantic Monthly* for a new magazine, 1857. It is still published in 1991.

RICHARD STRAUSS,
German composer, writes the opera *Ariadne auf Naxos*, 1912.

CARL SANDBURG
writes the biography *Lincoln: The Prairie Years*, 1926.

HENRY WADSWORTH LONGFELLOW,
having left his professorship at Harvard to pursue writing, publishes *The Song of Hiawatha*, 1855.

PIERRE TRUDEAU
becomes prime minister of Canada before his forty-ninth birthday, 1968. Trudeau became an international media superstar as "Trudeaumania" swept Canada.

WASSILY KANDINSKY,
a Russian painter who had studied in Munich and worked in Germany, returns to Russia a celebrity, 1914.

CHRISTOPH WILLIBALD GLUCK
composes the early opera masterpiece *Orfeo ed Euridice* ("Orpheus and Eurydice"), 1762. This was the first opera in Gluck's "reform" movement, wherein music was an integral part of plot development in opera and not merely a showcase for performers.

BENJAMIN FRANKLIN
suggests a voluntary union of the thirteen British colonies in North America, 1754. Canada was still largely under French rule.

HANS CHRISTIAN OERSTED
of Denmark isolates aluminum, 1825.

age forty-nine

"When I was as you are now, towering in the confidence of twenty-one, little did I suspect that I should be at forty-nine what I now am."
—Samuel Johnson

"The blush that flies at seventeen is fixed at forty-nine."
—Rudyard Kipling

GROVER CLEVELAND,
president of the United States, marries Frances Folsom, twenty-one, in the White House, 1886.

GEORGE GOETHALS
is appointed by President Theodore Roosevelt to complete the Panama Canal, 1907.

HUMPHREY BOGART
stars in the film *The Treasure of the Sierra Madre*, 1948.

ANTHONY QUINN
stars in the film *Zorba the Greek*, 1964.

HOWARD CARTER,
British archaeologist, discovers the tomb of King Tutankhamen, 1922.

LUCILLE BALL
divorces Desi Arnaz, 1960.

THOMAS MANN,
German novelist, writes *The Magic Mountain*, 1924.

SAMUEL GRAVELY, JR.,
is the first African-American admiral in the United States
Navy, 1971.

RICHARD NIXON
loses his bid for governor of California, 1962.

CZAR NICHOLAS II
of Russia abdicates, 1917. He was executed the following
year.

SHIRLEY MACLAINE
wins the 1983 Best Actress Academy Award for *Terms of
Endearment*.

COUNT LEO TOLSTOY
completes the classic *Anna Karenina*, 1877.

SIR WALTER SCOTT
writes *Ivanhoe*, 1820.

JOHANN STRAUSS, JR.,
composes *Die Fledermaus*, 1874.

DAN RATHER
makes his television news anchor debut on the "CBS
Evening News," March 9, 1981.

CLARA BARTON,
founder of the American Red Cross, travels to Europe to
provide care for soldiers in the Franco-Prussian War,
1870.

W. SOMERSET MAUGHAM
publishes *Of Human Bondage*, his first widely acclaimed work, 1915.

LOUIS BRANDEIS
is the first Jewish-American justice of the United States Supreme Court, 1916.

THERESIA VON PARADIS,
although blind, opens a school of music in Vienna, 1808. She was so admired by Mozart that he composed his Piano Concerto No. 18 in B-flat Minor in her honor.

KENNETH GRAHAME
writes the children's classic *The Wind in the Willows*, 1908.

THE CHEVALIER DE LAMARCK
begins studying fossils and becomes the "father of invertebrate paleontology," 1793.

ARTHUR MILLER
writes the play *After the Fall*, a painful account of his marriage to Marilyn Monroe, 1965.

HENRI ROUSSEAU
takes early retirement from the French Customs Service to pursue his second career as a painter, 1893.

age fifty

"A man is sane morally at thirty, rich mentally at forty, wise spiritually at fifty or never."
—Sir William Osler, Canadian surgeon

"The years between fifty and seventy are the hardest. You are always being asked to do things and yet are not decrepit enough to turn them down."
—T. S. Eliot

"Love is lame at fifty years."
—Thomas Hardy

"Youth is a malady of which one becomes cured a little every day."
—Mussolini, on his 50th birthday.

IRVING BERLIN
publishes the song "God Bless America," which he had written twenty-one years earlier, 1938.

FRANKLIN DELANO ROOSEVELT
is elected president of the United States, 1932.

WILLIAM HARVEY
of England publishes his findings on the circulation of the blood, 1628.

DANIEL BOONE,
having registered his Missouri land claims with the Spanish, loses title to all of them as the region becomes American territory, 1784.

EDWARD GIBBON
completes *The Rise and Fall of the Roman Empire*, 1787.

ROBERT BADEN POWELL
founds the Boy Scouts, 1907.

CHARLES DARWIN
publishes *The Origin of Species*, 1859.

LARRY MCMURTRY
wins the 1986 Pulitzer Prize in fiction for *Lonesome Dove*.

COLIN POWELL
is the first African-American to serve as National Security Adviser to the president of the United States, 1987.

JOHN UPDIKE
wins the 1982 Pulitzer Prize in fiction for *Rabbit Is Rich*.

IGOR SIKORSKY
takes his first ride in his invention, the helicopter, 1939.

MIKE WALLACE
first appears in the television news series "60 Minutes," 1968.

JOHN STEINBECK
publishes *East of Eden*, 1952.

ANDREW YOUNG
is elected mayor of Atlanta, Georgia, 1982.

JOHN BUNYAN
writes *The Pilgrim's Progress*, one of the most influential works ever published in English, 1678. Bunyan wrote much of it while serving a sentence in England's Bedford County Gaol as a religious dissenter.

ERASMUS,
one of the great Renaissance scholars, publishes his
parallel-text Greek-Latin translation of the New Testament, 1517.

WILHELM ROENTGEN
discovers X rays, 1895.

CHARLES BRONSON
wins a Golden Globe Award as the World's Most Popular
Actor, 1970.

ALFRED, LORD TENNYSON,
publishes *The Idylls of the King*, his treatment of the
legend of King Arthur, 1859.

CHRISTO,
Bulgarian-born "packaging" artist, "wraps" the entire
Pont Neuf bridge in Paris, 1985.

JOHN LA FARGE
is hailed as America's first great muralist as he paints the
Great Mural at the Church of the Ascension, New York,
1885.

PETER ILYICH TCHAIKOVSKY
composes the opera *Pique Dame* ("The Queen of
Spades"), 1890.

FRANKLIN SCHAFFNER
wins the 1970 Best Director Academy Award for *Patton*.
Among the film's other awards was an Oscar for Best
Actor to George C. Scott, who refused it.

JEAN-JACQUES ROUSSEAU
writes his two most important philosophical works, *The
Social Contract* and *Emile*, 1762.

REMBRANDT VAN RIJN,
famous Dutch painter, declares bankruptcy, 1656.

LIONEL ROTHSCHILD
is the first Jew to sit in the British Parliament, 1858. He had been duly elected four times between 1847 and 1857, but was not allowed to take his seat as he refused to swear allegiance to Christianity. His key supporter in the fight was Benjamin Disraeli, a Jew who had converted to Anglicanism.

HENRY FORD
unveils the revolutionary Model T assembly line, 1913.

THOMAS JEFFERSON
resigns in anger as secretary of state over the refusal of Congress to impeach Treasury Secretary Alexander Hamilton for alleged financial improprieties, 1793.

VIGDIS FINNBOGADOTTIR
becomes president of Iceland, 1980, the world's first elected female head of state. While many women have served as elected heads of government, such as Golda Meir, Margaret Thatcher, etc., Mrs. Finnbogadottir is the first woman, other than a queen, to serve as a head of state.

CAPTAIN JAMES COOK,
sailing from Hawaii, reaches the western coast of North America, 1778.

CLAUDE MONET,
French impressionist painter, is financially successful enough to buy the house at Giverny that he had been renting, 1890. The house was where he would spend the rest of his life and paint many of his most notable works.

DR. ALBERT SABIN
develops the oral polio vaccine, 1956.

FRANK SINATRA
marries Mia Farrow, thirty years his junior, 1966.

age fifty-one

LINUS PAULING
of the United States wins the first of two Nobel Prizes—
this time for chemistry, 1952.

HENRIK IBSEN
of Norway wins worldwide recognition for his play *A
Doll's House*, 1879.

JAMES HOFFA,
president of the Teamsters union, is convicted of jury
tampering, 1964.

FRANCES PERKINS
is the first woman to serve in the U.S. cabinet, 1933. She
was appointed secretary of labor by President Franklin
Roosevelt.

ABRAHAM LINCOLN
is elected president of the United States, 1860.

ANDRE MARIE AMPERE
discovers the laws of electromagnetism, 1826.

AARON BURR,
former vice-president of the United States, is acquitted
of treason, 1807.

VOLTAIRE,
French philosopher, is elected to the French Academy, 1746.

SANDRA DAY O'CONNOR
is the first woman justice of the United States Supreme Court, 1981.

SAMUEL F. B. MORSE,
after a decade of poverty and struggle, has a well-publicized demonstration of the telegraph underwater in New York City, 1842. The line is ripped out by the anchor of a passing ship and the demonstration is a humiliating failure.

DUSTIN HOFFMAN
wins the 1988 Best Actor Academy Award for *Rain Man*.

JOHN TYLER
succeeds to the presidency upon the death of President William Henry Harrison, 1841.

CHESTER A. ARTHUR
succeeds to the presidency upon the death of President James Garfield, 1881.

WILLIAM HOWARD TAFT,
who never wanted to be president, is inaugurated, 1909. Taft was reluctant to accept the Republican nomination. His real interest was the Supreme Court.

CALVIN COOLIDGE
succeeds to the presidency upon the death of President Warren G. Harding, 1923. He was given the oath of office by his father, a justice of the peace.

PETER ILYICH TCHAIKOVSKY
visits the United States, 1891 where he conducts at the inaugural concert at Carnegie Hall.

FRANKLIN D. ROOSEVELT
is inaugurated as president of the United States, 1933. He is the last president to have been inaugurated in March rather than on January 20, as is now the case.

MARGARET CHASE SMITH
is elected to the U.S. Senate from Maine, 1948. A Republican, she is the first woman to ever serve in both the House of Representatives and the Senate.

THOMAS HARDY
writes *Tess of the D'Urbervilles*, 1891.

SIDNEY POLLACK
wins the 1985 Best Director Academy Award for *Out of Africa*.

GOTTLIEB DAIMLER
builds the first motorcycle, 1885.

SIR EDWARD ELGAR's
Symphony No. 1 is first performed at Manchester, December 3, 1908. The symphony contains the song "The Land of Hope and Glory," which had first appeared in 1901. It became popular after King Edward VII heard Symphony No. 1 and suggested putting words to it, making the song almost a second national anthem of Great Britain.

age fifty-two

WILLIAM SHAKESPEARE
dies, 1616.

HUMPHREY BOGART
wins the 1951 Best Actor Academy Award for *The African Queen*.

ABRAHAM LINCOLN
is inaugurated as president of the United States, 1861.

GENERAL COLIN POWELL
is the first African-American chairman of the Joint Chiefs of Staff, 1989.

NAPOLEON BONAPARTE
dies of stomach cancer in exile on the British island of St. Helena, off the coast of Africa, 1821.

HANS VON KALTENBORN
becomes the first national network radio news reporter and commentator, 1930.

EDWARD ARLINGTON ROBINSON,
virtually unknown before his fifties, publishes *Collected Poems*, including the well-known "Miniver Cheevy," 1921. President Theodore Roosevelt once secured a job in the Customs Service for Robinson when he was a destitute young poet.

JEFFERSON DAVIS
is elected president of the Confederate States of America, 1861.

MUHAMMAD
the Prophet flees persecution in Mecca and finds haven in Medina, 622. This flight is known as the "hejira" and is so important that the Muslim calendar begins with it.

CLEMENT C. MOORE
writes "The Night Before Christmas," 1838.

SIR JOHN A. MACDONALD
becomes the first prime minister of Canada following confederation, 1867.

ROBERT DUVALL
wins the 1984 Best Actor Academy Award for *Tender Mercies*.

PERCY FAITH
wins a Grammy Award for "Theme from *A Summer Place*," 1960.

DAMON RUNYON
writes *Guys and Dolls*, 1932.

EDDIE RICKENBACKER,
former World War I ace, is sent on an official mission by the U.S. War Department, 1942. His plane is forced down by the Japanese over the South Pacific, and he drifts in a raft for twenty-four days before being rescued.

SAMUEL F. B. MORSE
has virtually given up on his invention, the telegraph, when, in the last hours of session, Congress appropriates $30,000 for an experimental demonstration, 1843.

IBN SAUD
becomes King of Saudi Arabia, 1932.

PAUL ROBESON,
American actor and singer, has his passport revoked by
the U.S. State Department, 1950. Robeson was to have
traveled to Moscow to receive the Stalin Peace Prize.
Robeson, an American Communist, was finally allowed
to travel to the Soviet Union in 1958.

EDGAR GOODSPEED
produces *The New Testament: An American Translation*,
1921, one of the first translations of the Bible into contemporary language.

BERNARD MALAMUD
wins a Pulitzer Prize for *The Fixer*, 1967.

JAMES ARNESS
appears in his last episode of the television series
"Gunsmoke," ending a twenty year run, 1975.

JIMMY CARTER
is elected president of the United States, 1976.

RICHARD WAGNER,
German composer, writes both the libretto and music to
the opera *Tristan und Isolde*, 1865.

SUSAN B. ANTHONY,
pioneer advocate for women's rights, is arrested for vot-
ing, 1876.

MILOS FORMAN
wins the 1984 Best Director and Best Picture Academy
Awards for *Amadeus*.

IVAN BOESKY
is convicted of insider trading in the largest Wall Street scandal ever, 1986. He pleaded guilty, was ordered to pay a $100 million fine, and was barred for life from trading securities.

CLARA BARTON
organizes the American Red Cross, 1873.

ALEXANDER SOLZHENITSYN
of the Soviet Union wins the 1970 Nobel Prize in literature.

ANTONIN DVORAK's
New World Symphony debuts, 1893. The Czech composer had lived and worked in both Iowa and New York, thus developing an interest in American folk-music forms reflected in this symphony.

GOTTLIEB DAIMLER
builds his first automobile, 1886. This was the first gasoline engine, self-propelled vehicle ever.

age fifty-three

MOHANDAS GANDHI
is sentenced to six years in prison for nationalist activity against the British colonial government in India, 1922.

ROBERT PEARY
arrives at the North Pole, 1909.

ADMIRAL KARL DOENITZ
becomes the last führer of Nazi Germany upon the suicide of Adolf Hitler, 1945.

VACLAV HAVEL,
celebrated Czech playwright previously imprisoned for human-rights activity, is elected president of the newly democratic Czechoslovakia, 1989.

MICHAEL CAINE
wins the 1986 Best Supporting Actor Academy Award for *Hannah and Her Sisters*.

RONALD REAGAN
appears as the villain in his last motion picture, *The Killers*, 1964.

SAMUEL F. B. MORSE
—at last—successfully demonstrates the telegraph, sending the message "What God Hath Wrought!" between Baltimore and Washington, D.C., 1844.

MARGARET THATCHER
is the first woman to serve as prime minister of Great Britain, 1979.

E. B. WHITE
writes the children's classic *Charlotte's Web*, 1952.

CLAUDIUS
becomes emperor of Rome, A.D. 43. Ridiculed because of a speech impediment, he is the subject of Robert Graves's successful novels *I, Claudius* and *Claudius the God*.

EDWIN LAND
produces the first color self-developing camera, the Color Polaroid, 1962.

CORAZON AQUINO
is elected president of the Philippines, 1986.

MARIAN ANDERSON
is the first African-American to sing at New York's Metropolitan Opera, 1955.

HENRIK IBSEN,
of Norway, has his play *Ghosts* appear, 1881. Audiences were shocked by its frank treatment of the subject of venereal disease.

WALT DISNEY
launches his weekly television program "The Wonderful World of Disney," 1954.

GENERAL LEW WALLACE
writes *Ben Hur*, 1880.

SIMON INGERSOLL
invents the pneumatic rock drill, 1871.

PETER PAUL RUBENS,
known primarily today as a painter, negotiates a temporary peace between England and Spain, 1630.

JOHN CONSTABLE,
one of Britain's greatest landscape painters, is elected a full member of the British Royal Academy of Art by a margin of one vote, 1829.

age fifty-four

JOHANNA SPYRI
of Switzerland writes *Heidi*, 1881.

KENESAW MOUNTAIN LANDIS
is named the first commissioner of professional baseball, 1920, after it is learned that the 1919 World Series was fixed by players and gamblers.

FRANKLIN D. ROOSEVELT
is elected to a second term as president, 1936.

MARY BAKER EDDY,
founder of Christian Science, writes *Science and Health with Key to the Scriptures*, 1875.

ELBERT GARY,
for whom Gary, Indiana, is named, organizes the U.S. Steel Corporation, 1901.

BUDDY EBSEN
debuts as Jed Clampett in the television series "The Beverly Hillbillies," 1962.

REVEREND NORMAN VINCENT PEALE
writes the self-help classic *The Power of Positive Thinking*, 1952.

MICHAEL DUKAKIS
is nominated for president by the Democratic party. He was defeated by George Bush less than a week after his fifty-fifth birthday, 1988.

ELIZABETH PEABODY
establishes the first kindergarten in the United States, 1860.

MIKHAIL S. GORBACHEV
becomes general secretary of the Communist party of the Soviet Union, 1985, less than a month after his fifty-fourth birthday.

SIR WALTER SCOTT
declares bankruptcy. The Scottish author had lost a fortune during the 1825 business depression and was faced with $600,000 worth of debts in 1820 dollars—a fortune. He set himself to repay the debts in full and raised one third of it through writing.

H. G. WELLS
writes *The Outline of History*, 1920.

HENRY WADSWORTH LONGFELLOW
loses both his wife and his home in a fire, 1861.

MONTEZUMA II,
emperor of Mexico, is killed by his subjects as he pleads for them to surrender to the Spanish, 1520.

ALFRED KINSEY,
pioneer of the scientific study of sexuality, publishes the then-controversial *Sexual Behavior in the American Male*, 1948. Kinsey himself was hardly a swinger. He never dated before age twenty-seven, and he married his first steady girlfriend.

ERNEST HEMINGWAY
wins a 1953 Pulitzer Prize for *The Old Man and the Sea*.

WALTER HOUSER BRATTAIN
of the U.S. wins a 1956 Nobel Prize in recognition of his
leadership of the team that invented the transistor.

LEONARDO DA VINCI
works under the patronage of King Louis XII, of France,
in Milan, 1506.

THEODORE DREISER
writes *An American Tragedy*, 1925.

HENRIK IBSEN,
Norway's greatest playwright, writes *An Enemy of the
People*, 1882. This play poses the problem of an individ-
ual who is right in a society that is wrong.

WALT DISNEY
opens Disneyland at Anaheim, California, 1955.

LUDWIG VAN BEETHOVEN
writes his Ninth Symphony, which contains the popular
"Ode to Joy," 1824.

WILLIAM CROOKES
of Great Britain discovers that certain elements have iso-
topes, 1898.

MARTIN VAN BUREN
is inaugurated as president of the United States, 1837.

RUTHERFORD B. HAYES
is inaugurated as president of the United States, 1877.

WILLIAM MCKINLEY
is inaugurated as president of the United States, 1897.

HERBERT HOOVER
is inaugurated as president of the United States, 1929.

age fifty-five

OTTO VON BISMARCK
becomes chancellor of the recently united German Empire, 1871.

ANDREW JOHNSON
succeeds to the presidency upon the death of President Lincoln, 1865.

WARREN G. HARDING
is inaugurated as president of the United States, 1921.

BENJAMIN HARRISON,
whose grandfather, William Henry Harrison has also been a president, is inaugurated, 1889.

GROVER CLEVELAND
is inaugurated as president the second time, 1883.

IVAN PAVLOV
of Russia wins the 1904 Nobel Prize in medicine for his studies of stimulus and response in dogs.

THE COMTE DE ROCHAMBEAU
arrives with the first French troops to support the American Revolution, 1780.

BENITO JUAREZ,
a full-blooded Indian, becomes president of Mexico,
1861.

JOHN D. ROCKEFELLER
retires from active control of Standard Oil, 1894.

MARLON BRANDO
appears in the film *Apocalypse Now* as Kurtz, the insane
head of a private army, 1979.

FRANK SINATRA
announces his retirement from the entertainment business, 1971. He is still entertaining in 1991.

RONALD REAGAN
is elected governor of California, 1966.

LYNDON BAINES JOHNSON
succeeds to the presidency upon the death of President
Kennedy, 1963.

LEE MARVIN,
American actor, is sued for half his fortune by a woman
with whom he had lived for six years, but never married.
The suit was unsuccessful, 1979.

THE CHEVALIER DE LAMARCK
begins writing a weather journal, 1799. He is the pioneer
of modern meteorology and gave the names "cumulus,"
"nimbus," "cirrus," etc. to the various types of clouds.

DICK HAYMES,
American popular singer, files bankruptcy a second time,
1971.

ALESSANDRO VOLTA
of Italy builds the first electric battery, 1800.

QUEEN LILIUOKALANI,
the last queen of Hawaii, is deposed, 1893.

age fifty-six

ABRAHAM LINCOLN
is assassinated on Good Friday, 1865. Only a month earlier, Andrew Johnson, Lincoln's running mate, was inaugurated as vice-president. Johnson was recovering from typhoid fever and drank whiskey to brace himself. By the time of the inauguration, Johnson was absolutely drunk and gave a rambling, silly speech. Although Lincoln defended him, the charges of drunkenness plagued Johnson throughout his term of office and were an important part of the impeachment proceedings against him in 1867. There really isn't any conclusive evidence that Johnson was an alcoholic.

AARON BURR,
former vice-president of the United States, having fled the country, returns to the United Sates under an assumed name and begins a lucrative law practice, 1812.

REX HARRISON
appears on film as Dr. Henry Higgins in the film *My Fair Lady*, based on George Bernard Shaw's play *Pygmalion*, 1964.

GEORGE BERNARD SHAW
writes *Pygmalion*, the basis of the 1964 film *My Fair Lady*, 1912.

DR. SEUSS
writes *Green Eggs and Ham*, 1960.

LUDWIG VAN BEETHOVEN
dies during an unseasonal thunderstorm, 1826. His last
action was to shake his fist at the sky.

JOHN WAYNE,
American actor, has a cancerous lung removed, 1963.

CHARLEMAGNE
is crowned king of the Holy Roman Empire, 800.

GEORG FRIEDRICH HANDEL
composes the *Messiah*, 1741.

THOMAS MANN,
one of the greatest twentieth-century German authors,
flees the Nazis, 1933.

BARBARA WALTERS
hosts her fiftieth television special, 1987.

RICHARD NIXON
is inaugurated as president of the United States, 1969.

WOODROW WILSON
is inaugurated as president of the United States, 1913.

VICTOR FLEMING
wins the 1939 Best Director Academy Award for *Gone
With the Wind*.

PABLO PICASSO
paints *Guernica*, a tribute to the memory of the city destroyed by Francisco Franco's fascist troops, 1937.

HENRY FORD
buys out all other stockholders in the Ford Motor Company, 1919.

WILLIAM PENN,
founder of Pennsylvania, is jailed in England on a trumped-up charge of debt, 1701.

LUCRETIA MOTT
and Elizabeth Cady Stanton hold the Women's Rights Convention of 1848.

SPIRO T. AGNEW,
vice-president of the United States, resigns after pleading no contest to charges of income tax evasion on bribes taken while he was governor of Maryland, 1973.

JAWAHARLAL NEHRU,
Indian nationalist leader and future prime minister, leaves prison the last time, 1945.

VOLTAIRE,
French philosopher, moves to the residence of King Frederick the Great of Prussia to serve as court philosopher, 1750.

GENERAL NORMAN SCHWARZKOPF
leads the allied forces in Operation Desert Storm, 1991.

THOMAS HARDY
writes *Jude the Obscure*, 1895.

JAMES J. HILL
completes the Great Northern Railway, which links the Great Lakes with the Pacific Northwest, 1893.

ROBERT A. MILLIKAN
of the United States wins the 1923 Nobel Prize for physics.

RICHARD WAGNER,
German composer, writes the libretto and music for *Die Meistersinger von Nürnberg*, 1868.

DR. SELMAN WAKSMAN
of the United States leads the team that discovers the antibiotic streptomycin, 1943.

RACHEL CARSON
writes *Silent Spring*, 1962. This book, which warned of the environmental dangers of pesticides, was an important beginning of the modern environmental movement.

MOSES MAIMONIDES,
a Jewish philosopher, lawyer, and personal physician to the sultan at Cairo, writes *The Guide for the Perplexed*, an exposition of the Jewish faith, 1190.

AKIHITO
becomes emperor of Japan, 1989.

age fifty-seven

CARLO COLLODI
writes *The Adventures of Pinocchio*, 1883. Although primarily remembered today for this book, the author was also a distinguished soldier and advocate of the unification of Italy.

NORMAN MAILER
wins a 1980 Pulitzer Prize for *The Executioner's Song*.

LINUS PAULING,
Nobel laureate, presents an international petition for peace and disarmament, 1958.

DASHIELL HAMMETT,
author of *The Thin Man* and *The Maltese Falcon*, is identified as an alleged Communist by the House Un-American Activities Committee, 1951.

MAO TSE-TUNG
is leader of the new People's Republic of China, 1949.

GENERAL GEORGE S. PATTON
leads the American Western Task Force into Morocco, 1942.

MIGUEL HIDALGO,
a Catholic priest, leads the struggle for Mexican independence from Spain, 1810.

SIR ISAAC NEWTON
is elected to the Royal Society, 1699.

HUMPHREY BOGART
undergoes surgery for a cancerous esophagus, 1956.

RICHARD WAGNER,
German composer, conducts the first complete performance of his operatic *Ring* cycle, 1870.

DR. MICHAEL DEBAKEY
successfully implants the first artificial heart, 1966.

ANNA SEWELL
writes the children's classic horse story, *Black Beauty*, 1877.

SIR ROBERT L. BORDEN
becomes prime minister of Canada, 1911. Borden served as prime minister during World War I and faced one of the most important crises in Canadian history. British Canadians were eager for conscription for military service in World War I as part of a united British Empire effort. French Canadians, on the other hand, opposed conscription. Borden's portrait appears on the Canadian $100 bill.

ALEXANDRE GUSTAVE EIFFEL
builds what was then the world's tallest structure, the Eiffel Tower, Paris, 1889. Construction required seven thousand tons of iron and steel to build the 984-foot-high tower.

ABRAHAM GESNER
first manufactures kerosene, 1854. Kerosene was the earliest important petroleum product.

ANGELA LANSBURY
stars in the television series, "Murder, She Wrote,"
1983.

age fifty-eight

GENERAL ROBERT E. LEE,
commander of the Confederate army of Northern Virginia, surrenders to Union General Ulysses S. Grant, forty-three, ending the Civil War, 1865.

FRANKLIN ROOSEVELT
is the first president ever elected to a third term, 1940.

CHARLES DICKENS
dies from overwork, 1870.

INGMAR BERGMAN,
Swedish film director, has probably the worst year of his life, 1976. He is arrested by Stockholm police for tax evasion during the middle of a rehearsal at the Royal Dramatic Theater. Shortly thereafter, he is hospitalized following a nervous breakdown.

JOHN HOLLAND,
Irish-American engineer, builds the first modern submarine, 1898.

MARY BAKER EDDY,
establishes the First Church of Christ, Scientist, Boston, 1879.

MIGUEL DE CERVANTES,
writing in prison, begins *Don Quixote*, 1605.

GIUSEPPE VERDI,
Italian operatic composer, writes *Aida*, 1871. Although it is commonly believed that the opera was composed in honor of the opening of the Suez Canal, this is not true, as the canal opened in 1869.

JAMES RAMSAY MACDONALD
is elected the first Labour prime minister of Great Britain, 1924.

JOAN CRAWFORD
costars in the thriller *Whatever Happened to Baby Jane?*, 1962.

JETHRO TULL,
English horticulturalist, writes a book urging farmers to plant seeds in rows rather than to scatter them, as was customary at the time, 1732.

CHARLES MACKINTOSH
bonds rubber to fabric, creating the first waterproof raincoat, 1824.

GENERAL ANTONIO LOPEZ DE SANTA ANNA,
victor of the Battle of the Alamo, declares himself President for Life of Mexico, 1853. He was deposed two years later.

JAWAHARLAL NEHRU
is the first prime minister of independent India, 1947.

JAMES MONROE
is inaugurated as president of the United States, 1817.

HENRIK IBSEN
writes the play *The Wild Duck*, 1884.

NORMAN LEAR
produces a parody of American soap operas, "Mary Hartman, Mary Hartman," 1976.

DAVID LIVINGSTONE,
Scottish medical missionary and African explorer, is greeted by Henry M. Stanley with the words "Dr. Livingstone, I presume," 1871.

JOHN LOCKE,
British philosopher, writes the influential *An Essay Concerning Human Understanding*, 1690.

MIKHAIL S. GORBACHEV,
president of the Soviet Union, wins the 1990 Nobel Peace Prize.

POPE JOHN PAUL II,
born Karol Wojtyla in Poland, is the first non-Italian pope in 456 years, 1979.

AUGUSTE RODIN
sculpts *The Kiss*, which is deemed too erotic by the critics, 1899.

L. DOUGLAS WILDER
is elected governor of Virginia, the first African-American to ever serve as governor of a U. S. state, 1989.

WILLIAM SHOEMAKER,
perhaps the greatest jockey of all time, retires after forty years. He is the first jockey in the history of horse racing to ride one thousand stakes winners in a career, 1989.

age fifty-nine

RICHARD NIXON
is reelected president of the United States, 1972.

CONRAD HILTON
organizes Hilton Hotel Systems, 1946.

BENJAMIN HARRISON,
president of the United States and grandson of President
William Henry Harrison, had one of the most tragic
weeks in his life, 1892. On October 25, his wife dies,
and he is defeated for reelection less than two weeks
later.

PIERRE TRUDEAU
is defeated as prime minister of Canada, 1979.

GAIL BORDEN
first commercially produces evaporated milk, 1860.

GERTRUDE STEIN
writes *The Autobiography of Alice B. Toklas*, 1933.

SIR RICHARD ATTENBOROUGH
wins the 1982 Best Director Academy Award for *Gandhi*.

SENECA,
Spanish-born writer, scholar, and orator, is appointed
adviser to the insane Roman emperor Nero, A.D. 59.

JOHN MILTON,
although completely blind, writes *Paradise Lost*, 1652.

FYODOR DOSTOYEVSKY
completes *The Brothers Karamazov*, 1880.

JOHN RUSKIN,
Britain's most influential art critic, is successfully sued
for libel by the American painter James Whistler, 1878.
Ruskin had accused Whistler of "flinging a pot of paint
in the public's face."

MARY WOLLSTONECRAFT SHELLEY
writes the novel *Frankenstein*, 1818.

MIKHAIL SHOLOKHOV
of the Soviet Union wins the 1965 Nobel Prize for literature.

VIOLETTA BARROS DE CHAMORRO
defeats Sandinista leader Daniel Ortega in the free Nic-
araguan elections of 1989.

age sixty

"You make me chuckle when you say that you are no longer young, that you have turned twenty-four. A man is or may be young to after sixty, and not old before eighty."
> —Oliver Wendell Holmes, Jr., *The Mind and Faith of Justice Holmes*, by Max Lerner

"Spring still makes spring in the mind
When sixty years are told;
Love makes anew the throbbing heart
and we are never old."
> —Ralph Waldo Emerson

"After a man passes sixty, his mischief is chiefly in his head."
> —Ed Howe

"The uselessness of men above sixty years of age and the incalculable benefit it would be in commercial, in political, and in professional life, if as a matter of course, men stopped work at this age."
> —Sir William Osler (age fifty-six), Canadian surgeon

"I'm growing old, I've sixty years . . ."
> —Gustave Nadaud, French poet

MOHANDAS GANDHI
leads followers on a two-hundred-mile march to the sea to protest the British colonial government monopoly on salt, 1930.

MARK TWAIN,
having made some very poor investments, finds himself $100,000 in debt and considers bankruptcy, 1896. However, a successful lecture tour schedule helps him repay every penny. Twain had suffered serious financial worries for over ten years, largely as a result of publishing his own works, unwise investments, and his own generosity to others.

VICTOR HUGO
writes *Les Misérables*, 1862.

SAUL BELLOW
wins a Pulitzer Prize for *Humboldt's Gift*, 1975.

ROCK HUDSON,
U.S. actor, dies of AIDS, 1985.

JUAN PERON,
dictator of Argentina, is deposed, 1955.

PIERRE TRUDEAU
is reelected as Canada's prime minister, 1979.

LOUIS ST. LAURENT,
future prime minister of Canada, begins his career in politics by being elected to Parliament, 1942.

HARRY S TRUMAN
succeeds to the presidency on the death of President Franklin Roosevelt, less than a month before his sixty-first birthday, 1945.

LOUIS PASTEUR
begins his study of rabies, 1882.

GERALDINE PAGE
wins the 1984 Best Actress Academy Award for *The Trip to Bountiful*.

ARCHBISHOP THOMAS CRANMER
drafts the *Book of Common Prayer*, 1545.

GENERAL WINFIELD SCOTT
leads U.S. forces in the Mexican War of 1846.

IZAAK WALTON,
English writer and fishing enthusiast, publishes *The Compleat Angler*, 1653.

HELMUT KOHL,
chancellor of West Germany since 1982, is elected the first chancellor of reunited Germany, 1990.

T. S. ELIOT,
American-born British poet, wins the 1948 Nobel Prize in literature.

PERCIVAL LOWELL,
American astronomer, writes *Memoirs on a Trans-Neptunian Planet*, 1915. In this book, he accurately predicted the location of the then-undiscovered planet Pluto. It would be discovered by Clyde Tombaugh in 1930.

FRED ASTAIRE
has a good year, 1959. He wins good reviews for his first dramatic acting role in *On the Beach* and his television special "An Evening with Fred Astaire" wins nine Emmy Awards.

DOM PERIGNON,
a French monk, makes his first batch of champagne, 1698.

THOMAS JEFFERSON,
president of the United States, makes the Louisiana Purchase, acquiring the region from the Mississippi River to the Rocky Mountains, 1803.

EDWARD VII,
Prince of Wales, becomes king on the death of his
mother, Queen Victoria, 1901.

MAX PLANCK
of Germany wins the 1918 Nobel Prize in physics.

PAUL CEZANNE,
a French painter known for his eccentricity and fussi-
ness, takes a hundred sittings to complete a portrait of
Ambroise Vollard, 1899.

age sixty-one

"Within I do not find wrinkles and need heart, but unspent youth."
          —Ralph Waldo Emerson (age sixty-one)

RICHARD NIXON
resigns from the presidency, 1974.

PAUL NEWMAN
wins the Best Actor Academy Award for *The Color of Money*, 1986.

CLARENCE DAY
writes *Life with Father*, 1935.

SYDNEY GREENSTREET
appears in *The Maltese Falcon*, 1941.

GEORGE ARLISS
wins the 1929 Best Actor Academy Award for *Disraeli*.

OLIVER WENDELL HOLMES, JR.,
is appointed associate justice of the U.S. Supreme Court, 1902.

P. T. BARNUM
produces his first circus, the Greatest Show on Earth, 1871.

SIR ISAAC NEWTON
is elected president of Britain's Royal Society, 1703.

LEON TROTSKY
is assassinated in Mexico on Stalin's orders, 1940.

GERALD R. FORD
becomes president of the United States, 1974. He is the
first U.S. president who was never elected vice-president
or president, but was confirmed by the Senate as vice-
president on the resignation of Spiro Agnew, 1973. He
succeeded to the presidency on the resignation of Richard Nixon.

ANDREW JACKSON
is inaugurated as president of the United States, 1829.

JOHN ADAMS
is inaugurated as president of the United States, 1797.

SAUL BELLOW
wins the 1976 Nobel Prize in literature.

LINUS PAULING
wins his second Nobel Prize, this time for peace, 1962.
Pauling had been a strong advocate of nuclear disarmament and had presented an international peace petition
to the United Nations.

CARL SANDBURG
completes the biography *Lincoln: The War Years*, 1939.

ALBERT EINSTEIN
becomes a U.S. citizen, 1940.

THE MARQUIS DE SADE,
pornographer and source of the words ''sadism'' and
''sadistic,'' is committed to the insane asylum at Charenton, France, 1801.

DR. BARNEY CLARK,
a retired dentist, is the first recipient of a permanent artificial heart, the Jarvik-7, 1982.

age sixty-two

FRANKLIN D. ROOSEVELT
is elected to a fourth term as president of the United States, 1944.

DWIGHT D. EISENHOWER
is elected president of the United States, 1962.

HENRIK IBSEN
writes the classic play *Hedda Gabler*, 1890.

BENITO MUSSOLINI,
deposed dictator of Italy, is shot while trying to flee the country with his mistress, Clara Petacci, 1943.

CHARLES DARWIN
publishes his most controversial work, applying scientific evolution to humans, *The Descent of Man*, 1871.

JOHN WAYNE
wins the 1969 Academy Award for Best Actor for *True Grit*.

HENRI DUNANT,
founder of the International Red Cross, is found destitute, living in an almshouse, 1890.

ULYSSES S. GRANT
declares bankruptcy, 1884. The former president had left the White House with over $100,000. However, Grant had invested his money with his son and a corrupt partner, Frederick Ward. When the investment banking house of Grant and Ward failed, the elder Grant was wiped out. Fortunately, the writer Mark Twain took an interest in Grant's plight (Twain, incidentally, was a Confederate veteran), and the kindhearted writer published Grant's memoirs out of his own pocket, netting the Grant family some $500,000 and a negligible amount for Twain. Grant died the next year.

WOODROW WILSON,
president of the United States, suffers a debilitating stroke, 1919. It is believed that his second wife, the former Edith Bolling Galt, actually carried out the day-to-day responsibilities of the presidency. A former Washington socialite, the second Mrs. Wilson was the butt of a classic Washington joke: "What did Mrs. Galt do when the president proposed to her? She was so surprised, she fell out of bed."

COUNT ZEPPELIN
test flies his airship over Lake Constance, Germany, 1902.

CARL SANDBURG
wins a 1940 Pulitzer Prize for his Lincoln biography series.

COUNT LEO TOLSTOY
renounces his wealth and land holdings in order to live among the peasants, 1890. His children were opposed to the idea.

JOHN MITCHELL,
former attorney general of the United States, is found
guilty of covering up the Watergate Affair, 1975.

J.R.R. TOLKIEN
publishes *The Lord of the Rings*, 1954–56.

age sixty-three

ROBERT E. LEE
dies, 1870.

THOMAS HOBBES,
British philosopher, writes the political-science classic
Leviathan, 1651.

BENJAMIN O. DAVIS, SR.,
is the first African-American general in the United States
Army, 1940.

DAVID DINKINS
is the first African-American to be elected mayor of New
York City, 1990.

SIR ISAAC NEWTON
is knighted by Queen Anne, 1705.

PAUL EHRLICH,
German physician, wins the 1908 Nobel Prize in medicine for his studies of the human immune system.

FRANCIS GALTON
of England, a first cousin of Charles Darwin, studies the
individual characteristics of fingerprints and suggests
their use as a means of positive identification, 1885.

ALISTAIR COOKE
becomes host of "Masterpiece Theatre" on Public Television, 1971.

GUTZON BORGLUM
begins work on Mount Rushmore, 1930.

SAMUEL BECKETT,
Irish author working in France, wins the 1969 Nobel Prize in literature.

EDGAR DEGAS,
French painter, completely loses his sight, 1897.

age sixty-four

FERDINAND DE LESSEPS
of France directs the completion of the Suez Canal, 1869.

WALTER CRONKITE
retires as anchor of the "CBS Evening News," March 1981.

AUGUSTE RODIN
sculpts his best-known work, *The Thinker*, 1904.

CLAUDE MONET,
father of impressionism, paints the celebrated *Waterlilies*, 1904.

HENRY FORD
introduces the Model A automobile, 1927.

FRANCISCO SUAREZ,
Jesuit priest and philosopher, is one of the first to question the theory of the divine right of kings. Suarez also criticized the Spanish colonial treatment of the Indians, 1612.

GEORGE BUSH
is inaugurated as president of the United States, 1989.

EUDORA WELTY
wins a Pulitzer Prize for *The Optimist's Daughter*, 1973.

MARTIN VAN BUREN,
former president of the United States, is nominated for
president by the antislavery Free Soil party. A Democratic president from 1837 to 1841, Van Buren took so
many votes from the Democratic nominee that the Whig
party candidate, Zachary Taylor, won the election, 1848.

CHARLES CHAPLIN
is refused entry into the United States because of his
political views, 1933.

GEORGE RAFT,
American actor, who often boasted of his ties to the underworld, experiences one of the most difficult periods
of his life, 1958–59. Raft invested heavily in his own
television series, which failed, the Internal Revenue Service demanded back taxes, and the new Castro regime
seized his Havana casino. Nonethless, Raft lived on to
age eighty-five.

WILLIAM HOWARD TAFT,
former president of the United States, finally gets his
dream job—chief justice of the Supreme Court, 1921. Taft
never wanted to be president and once said, "The truth
is, I don't ever remember being president." He told his
successor, Woodrow Wilson, that he was "glad to
leave." Taft was our heaviest president and heaviest chief
justice, weighing over three hundred pounds. When he
moved into the White House, a new bathtub had to be
installed to accommodate him. He fit the stereotype of
a heavyset person, as he was jolly, kind, honest, and
easygoing. A newspaper reporter once said that Taft
reminded him of "an American bison—a jolly, kind
one."

MARGARET THATCHER
resigns as prime minister of Great Britain, 1990.

PIERRE TRUDEAU
resigns as prime minister of Canada and retires from politics, 1984.

ZACHARY TAYLOR
is inaugurated as president of the United States, 1849. A strict Episcopalian, Taylor did not immediately learn of his nomination, as he refused to accept the message, which was brought on Sunday.

age sixty-five

"I'm sixty-five, and I guess that puts me in with the geriatrics. But if there were fifteen months in a year, I would only be forty-eight."
—James Thurber

VOLTAIRE,
French philosopher, writes *Candide*, 1759.

RONALD REAGAN
unsuccessfully challenges President Ford for the Republican nomination for president, 1976.

UPTON SINCLAIR
wins a 1945 Pulitzer Prize for *Dragon's Teeth*.

MARY LOU WILLIAMS,
jazz pioneer and convert to Catholicism, composes her *Mass*, which is performed at Saint Patrick's Cathedral, New York, 1975.

LAURA INGALLS WILDER
begins her literary career by publishing her first book *Little House in the Big Woods*, the first of her successful *Little House on the Prairie* series, 1932.

JOHN QUINCY ADAMS
is the only former president of the United States to serve in the U.S. House of Representatives. He was elected a congressman from Massachusetts, 1830.

JAMES BUCHANAN
is inaugurated as president of the United States, 1857.
Viewing the secession of the Southern states, Buchanan
remarked, "I am the last president of the United States."

retirement

"The worst of work nowadays is what happens to people when they cease work."

—G. K. Chesterton

"O blest retirement, friend to life's decline
Retreats from care, that never must be mine
How blest is he who crowns in shades like these
A youth of labor with an age of ease;
Who quits a world where strong temptations try
And, 'tis hard to combat, learns to fly."

—Oliver Goldsmith

"Multa ferunt anni venientes commoda secum, multa rece-
dentes adimunt." *("Many blessings do the advancing years*
bring with them, as they retire, they take away.")

—Horace

age sixty-six

PAUL EHRLICH,
German physician, develops an arsenic derivative that is
effective in the treatment of syphilis, 1911.

PAUL CEZANNE
paints *Les Grandes Beigneuses*, 1904.

JOSEPH HAYDN
composes the oratorio the *Creation*, 1798.

WINSTON CHURCHILL
becomes prime minister of Great Britain the first time,
1940.

PAUL VI
becomes pope, 1962.

MICHELANGELO
finishes painting *The Last Judgment*, 1541.

HERMAN MELVILLE,
author of *Moby Dick*, retires from his job with the U.S.
Customs Service, 1885.

DR. WILLIAM HINTON,
who had developed a blood test to detect syphilis, is the
first African-American professor of medicine at Harvard,
1948.

LOUIS ST. LAURENT,
after only six years in elective politics, is elected prime
minister of Canada, 1948.

NELSON A. ROCKEFELLER,
governor of New York and three-time candidate for the
Republican presidential nomination, is confirmed by the
Senate as vice-president of the United States, 1975.

age sixty-seven

GIUSEPPE GARIBALDI,
architect of the unification of Italy, is elected to the Italian Parliament, 1874. An interesting but little-known fact about him is that Abraham Lincoln invited him to command the Union forces in the American Civil War.

SPENCER TRACY
appears in his last film, *Guess Who's Coming to Dinner*, 1967.

GEORGE BERNARD SHAW
writes the play *Saint Joan*, 1923.

JIM WRIGHT,
speaker of the U.S. House of Representatives, resigns after questions of financial impropriety are raised, 1989.

INDIRA GANDHI,
prime minister of India and daughter of Nehru, is assassinated, 1984.

age sixty-eight

FRANCISCO GOYA,
Spanish painter, paints the poignant *Execution of 8 May 1808*, 1814, which depicts the execution of Spanish patriots by the occupying French.

CLARENCE DARROW
defends John Scopes in the Tennessee "Monkey" trial of 1825. Scopes was charged with violating a state statute that prohibited the teaching of evolution in public schools. Scopes was found guilty, but Darrow's eloquent defense led to a greater public tolerance of the theory of evolution.

GALILEO
is sentenced to prison by the Inquisition for advocating the Copernican theory—that the earth revolves around the sun and not vice versa, 1632.

CHARLES DE GAULLE
is elected president of France, 1958.

MATTHEW VASSAR
makes an endowment to establish Vassar College at Poughkeepsie, New York, 1861. By the time of his death in 1868, Vassar had contributed over $800,000 to the college.

QUEEN VICTORIA
celebrates the Diamond Jubilee, commemorating fifty years on the British throne, 1887.

JOHN WAYNE
appears in the film *Rooster Cogburn*, 1975.

ALEXANDER GRAHAM BELL
calls his former laboratory assistant Thomas Watson in the first transcontinental telephone call, from New York to San Francisco, 1915.

WILLIAM HENRY HARRISON
is inaugurated as president of the United States, 1841. He is most noted for the fact that he caught pneumonia during the inaugural parade and died within a month of taking office. Thus he served a shorter term of office than any other president.

age sixty-nine

JOHN WAYNE
appears in his last movie, *The Shootist*, 1976.

RONALD REAGAN
is inaugurated as president, 1981. He is the oldest man
ever to hold that office.

EDMUND GWENN
wins an Academy Award for his role as Santa Claus in
the Christmas classic film *Miracle on 34th Street*, 1947.

NICHOLAS MURRAY BUTLER,
president of Columbia University and influential Republican leader, wins the 1931 Nobel Peace Prize for his role
in establishing the Carnegie Endowment for International
Peace.

ED SULLIVAN
hosts the last "Ed Sullivan Show," 1971.

GEORGE BERNARD SHAW
wins the 1925 Nobel Prize for literature.

HERMANN HESSE
wins the 1946 Nobel Prize for literature.

ALEXANDER CALDER,
American mobile artist, creates the motorized mobile
Red, Black and Blue at the Dallas Airport, 1967.

BRIGHAM YOUNG,
Mormon leader, fathers the last of his children by his
twenty-seven wives, 1870. At his death in 1877, he was
survived by seventeen wives and forty-seven children.

VICTOR HUGO
is elected to the French National Assembly and resigns
in frustration, 1870.

JAN SMUTS
is elected prime minister of South Africa, 1939. Smuts
had a reputation as an international statesman, but his
opposition to strict apartheid at home proved his political
undoing.

JOSEPH HAYDN
composes the oratorio the *Seasons*, 1801.

KURT WALDHEIM
is elected president of Austria, 1988. The former United
Nations secretary general was the focus of an international controversy when questions were raised regarding
his role as a German officer during World War II. An
international panel examined the evidence and deter-
mined that although Waldheim himself had committed no
war crimes, it appeared likely that he knew of some.
Nonetheless, the people of Austria elected him.

CASEY STENGEL
manages the New York Yankees to an American League
pennant, but they lose the World Series to Pittsburgh,
1960.

age seventy

"I believe that one has to be seventy before one is full of courage. The young are always half-hearted."

—D. H. Lawrence

"Being over seventy is like being engaged in a war. All our friends are going or gone and we survive amongst the dead and dying on a battlefield."

—Muriel Spark

"To be seventy years young is sometimes far more cheerful than to be forty years old."
—Oliver Wendell Holmes, Sr., in a letter to Julia Ward Howe on her seventieth birthday, 1889.

"It is too late! Ah, nothing is too late
Till the tired heart shall cease to palpitate.
Cato learned Greek at eighty; Sophocles
Wrote his grand Oedipus, and Simonides
Bore off the prize of verse from his compeers,
When each had numbered more than forescore years . . .
Chaucer, at Woodstock with the nightingales,
At sixty wrote the Canterbury tales;
Goethe at Weimar, toiling to the last,
Completed Faust when eighty years were past.
These are indeed exceptions; but they show
How far the gulf-stream of our youth may flow
Into the arctic regions of our lives. . . .
FOR AGE IS OPPORTUNITY NO LESS
THAN YOUTH ITSELF though in another dress,
And as the evening twilight fades away
The sky is filled with stars invisible by day."

—Henry Wadsworth Longfellow

> *"In seventy or eighty years, a man may have a deep gust of the world; know what it is, what it can afford, and what 'tis to have been a man."*
> —Sir Thomas Browne, *Christian Morals*

ARTURO TOSCANINI
becomes musical director of the NBC Symphony Orchestra, 1937.

LIONEL BARRYMORE,
appears in the film *Key Largo*, 1948.

SIR JOSEPH LISTER
is made Baron Lister of Lyme Regis in honor of his achievements in medicine, the first medical man to be honored with a peerage, 1897.

HELEN HAYES,
American actress, wins the 1970 Best Supporting Actress Academy Award for *Airport*.

BENJAMIN DISRAELI
returns to office as prime minister, 1874.

POPE JULIUS II
lays the cornerstone of St. Peter's Basilica, Rome, 1513.

CORNELIUS VANDERBILT,
having made a fortune in the steamboat business, begins investing in railroads, which makes him one of the super-millionaires, 1847.

W. SOMERSET MAUGHAM
writes the novel of man's spiritual search *The Razor's Edge*, 1944.

NOAH WEBSTER
publishes his masterpiece, *An American Dictionary of the English Language*, 1828.

MARY CASSATT
has to give up painting as her eyesight fails, 1914.

FOUJITA,
Japanese-born French painter, converts to Catholicism
and takes the name Leonard, in honor of da Vinci, 1959.

EDMOND HOYLE
of England writes a rule book on the card game whist,
1742. He went on to write rule books for chess and other
games and is thus the source of the common expression
''according to Hoyle.''

age seventy-one

"Our machines have now been running seventy or eighty years, and we must expect that, worn as they are, here a pivot, there a wheel, now a pinion, next a spring will be giving way; and however we may tinker them up for a while, all will at length surcease motion."

—Thomas Jefferson, seventy-one, writing to
John Adams, seventy-nine, 1814

ALBEN BARKLEY
is elected vice-president of the United States, 1948. He is the oldest man to hold that office.

KONRAD ADENAUER
is elected leader of the German Christian Democratic party, 1947.

GEORGES P. VANIER
is appointed governor-general of Canada, 1959. The governor-general is the constitutional representative of Queen Elizabeth II. This is notable because Vanier, a French Canadian, was the first francophone and the first Roman Catholic to hold that office. Vanier, who had lost a leg during World War I, had served as ambassador to France. Vanier's appointment is ironic; Canada's allegiance to the British crown was the result of the defeat of the French in 1763.

JOHN HOUSEMAN
wins an Academy Award for Best Supporting Actor for the film *The Paper Chase*, 1973.

GENERAL DOUGLAS MACARTHUR
is relieved of duty as commander of the allied forces in
Korea, 1951.

GOLDA MEIR
becomes prime minister of Israel, 1969.

MICHELANGELO
is appointed architect of St. Peter's, Rome, 1546.

COUNT LEO TOLSTOY
writes *Resurrection*, 1899.

age seventy-two

"Old age isn't so bad when you consider the alternative."
— Maurice Chevalier, seventy-two,
The New York Times, October 9, 1960

W. AVERELL HARRIMAN
negotiates the Nuclear Test Ban Treaty, 1963.

SUSAN B. ANTHONY
is elected president of the American Women's Suffrage
Societies, 1892, a position she holds for eight years.

PRESIDENT FRANÇOIS MITTERRAND
of France begins a second seven-year term, 1988.

JOHN TYLER,
former president of the United States, is elected to the
Confederate House of Representatives, 1861.

MOHANDAS GANDHI
is jailed by the British for the last time, 1942.

THOMAS JEFFERSON,
former president of the United States, facing bankruptcy,
sells his 6,400-book library to pay his debts and feed
himself, 1815. These books were the basis of the Library
of Congress.

PATRICIO AYLWIN
is elected president of Chile, 1990. Aylwin is the first
democratically elected president of that country in seventeen years.

age seventy-three

ANTONIO GAUDI,
architect of the Church of the Holy Family in Barcelona,
which he had begun forty-four years earlier, is run over
by a streetcar and killed, 1926.

PETER MARK ROGET
completes his *Thesaurus*, 1852.

RONALD REAGAN
is elected to a second term as president of the United
States, 1984.

KONRAD ADENAUER
is elected the first chancellor of the German Federal Republic, 1949.

GIUSEPPE VERDI,
Italian composer, fascinated by Shakespeare, composes
Otello, based on the Shakespeare play *Othello*, 1887.

HERBERT HOOVER,
former president of the United States, is appointed chairman of the Commission on Organization of the Executive
Branch of Government, commonly known as the Hoover
Commission, 1947.

JOHN HUSTON
directs the film *The Man Who Would Be King*, 1975.

HENRI DUNANT,
founder of the International Red Cross, after filing bankruptcy and facing homelessness and complete destitution, wins the 1901 Nobel Peace Prize.

STUDS TERKEL,
American author, wins a Pulitzer Prize for *The Good War*, an account of World War II, 1985.

KING GEORGE III
of Great Britain, who had lost his North American colonies (except Canada) during the American Revolution, becomes hopelessly insane, 1811.

JAMES MONROE,
former president of the United States, dies on July 4, 1831, one of three presidents to die on Independence Day.

DENG XIAOPING
becomes undisputed ruler of China after purging the radical "Gang of Four," 1977.

KLAUS BARBIE,
former Gestapo chief at Lyons (France), is sentenced to life imprisonment, 1987.

KING CHARLES
of France is forced to abdicate after the Revolution of 1830.

HOKUSAI,
Japanese painter, is busy working on his *36 Views of Mount Fuji*, 1833.

FRANCISCO GOYA
enters his morbid Black Period of painting, characterized by grotesque, depressing subjects, 1819.

MADAME TUSSAUD
opens her London wax museum, 1834.

ALBERT EINSTEIN,
an American citizen born in Germany, is offered the presidency of Israel, but declines it, 1952.

WILLIAM WORDSWORTH
is appointed Poet Laureate of England, 1843. During his seven years in that post, he never wrote any poetry.

WILLIAM DURANT
declares bankruptcy, 1935. Durant, one of the organizers of General Motors Corporation, was one of the richest men in America after he sold his G.M. shares to the Du Pont Corporation in 1920. He speculated with his fortune on the stock market and lost virtually everything during the 1929 crash.

age seventy-four

KATHARINE HEPBURN
wins an Oscar for *On Golden Pond*, 1981.

A. PHILIP RANDOLPH,
a veteran civil rights leader who had organized the Pullman Porter strike of the 1920s, is one of the organizers of the 1963 civil rights march on Washington.

FERDINAND DE LESSEPS,
having directed the completion of the Suez Canal, begins the unsuccessful French attempt to build a Panama Canal, 1879.

ISAAC BASHEVIS SINGER,
Polish-born American writer in the Yiddish language, wins the 1978 Nobel Prize for literature.

LORENZO GHIBERTI
completes the bronze doors of the baptistry of the Cathedral of Santa Maria del Fiore, 1452, a task begun fifty years earlier.

age seventy-five

"I promise to keep on living as though I expected to live forever. Nobody grows old by merely living a number of years. People grow old by deserting their ideals. Years may wrinkle the skin, but to give up interest wrinkles the soul."
—General Douglas MacArthur, on his seventy-fifth
birthday, January 26, 1955

"Never get up with the lark. Get up only for a lark."
—Lord Boyd Orr, seventy-five, on his longevity,
Boston Herald, July 1, 1955

FRANK SINATRA
celebrates his seventy-fifth birthday, December 1990, by performing.

JAN SMUTS,
prime minister of South Africa, is the principal drafter of the Preamble to the United Nations Charter, 1945.

GENERAL WINFIELD SCOTT,
a hero of both the War of 1812 and the Mexican War, retires from the army, 1861. Scott, a Southerner, was asked to lead Confederate troops, but declined out of loyalty to the Union, 1861.

CHAIM WEITZMANN
is elected president of Israel, 1948.

LOUIS ST. LAURENT
retires as prime minister of Canada, 1957.

HELEN KELLER
writes *Teacher*, the story of Anne Sullivan Macy, the woman who taught the deaf and dumb child sign language, 1955. This book was the basis of the film *The Miracle Worker*.

VICTOR HUGO,
French novelist, writes *The Art of Being a Grandfather*, 1877.

CECIL B. DEMILLE
produces and directs his sound version of *The Ten Commandments*, 1956.

FRED ASTAIRE
appears in the film *The Towering Inferno* in a dramatic role and is nominated for an Academy Award for Best Supporting Actor, 1974.

MARC CHAGALL
designs the famous stained-glass windows for the synagogue at the Hadassah Hebrew Medical Center, 1962.

SIR JOHN A. MACDONALD,
Canada's first prime minister, is elected a third time, but dies from the exertion of the campaign, 1890.

HENRY FORD
is awarded the Order of the German Eagle by Nazi leader Hermann Göring on the occasion of Ford's seventy-fifth birthday, 1938. Ford was himself a notorious anti-Semite.

MICHELANGELO
paints *The Conversion of Saint Paul and the Crucifixion of Saint Peter*, 1550.

age seventy-six

RICHARD NIXON,
former president of the United States, travels to China after the Tiananmen Square massacre and meets with Chinese officials, 1989.

GOLDA MEIR
retires as prime minister of Israel, 1974.

BERNARD M. BARUCH
is appointed United States representative to the United Nations Atomic Energy Commission, 1946.

HENRY FONDA
wins the 1981 Best Actor Academy Award for *On Golden Pond*.

THOMAS JEFFERSON,
former president of the United States, establishes the University of Virginia, 1819.

EDWARD G. ROBINSON
appears in the science-fiction horror film *Soylent Green*, his last role, 1970.

KING VICTOR EMMANUEL III
of Italy abdicates, 1946. Nearly seventy-seven, the king witnessed the people of Italy reject the monarchy in a referendum.

ANNA MARY ROBERTSON MOSES,
known as "Grandma" Moses, takes up oil painting after
her fingers become too stiff for needlepoint, 1936. She
was acclaimed as one of America's best primitive painters, and this was the beginning of a twenty-five-year career ending with her death in 1961 at age 101.

GEORGES CLEMENCEAU
becomes prime minister of France for the second time,
1917. The French leader was one of the big four at the
Versailles Peace Conference of 1919 that also included
Woodrow Wilson of the United States, David Lloyd
George of Britain, and Vittorio Orlando of Italy.

age seventy-seven

"At seventy-seven, it is time to be earnest."
—Samuel Johnson

POPE JOHN XXIII,
reformist pope, who later presided over the historic Second Vatican Council, is elected, 1958.

SIR JOHN GIELGUD
wins the 1981 Academy Award for Best Supporting Actor for the comedy *Arthur*.

SAMUEL GOLDWYN
produces his last film, *Porgy and Bess*, 1959.

ELEANOR ROOSEVELT
is appointed U.S. delegate to the United Nations, 1961.

ALBERT SCHWEITZER
wins the 1952 Nobel Peace Prize.

WINSTON CHURCHILL
returns as prime minister of Great Britain, 1951.

GLORIA SWANSON,
silent film star, appears in her last film, *Airport 1975*, 1974.

LUIS BUNUEL,
surrealist filmmaker and associate of Salvador Dali, directs his last film, 1977.

RONALD REAGAN
retires from the White House, 1989.

CHARLES IVES
wins the 1951 Pulitzer Prize in music for his Third Symphony. Although Ives had retired from musical composition at age forty-four, his works were "discovered" by conductor and composer Leonard Bernstein.

DON AMECHE
wins the 1985 Academy Award for Best Supporting Actor for the film *Cocoon*.

age seventy-eight

FIELD MARSHAL PAUL VON HINDENBURG
is elected president of Germany, 1925.

IGNACE JAN PADEREWSKI,
Polish patriot and concert pianist, makes his last concert
tour of the United States, 1938.

MAE WEST
makes a film comeback in *Myra Breckenridge*, 1970.

JUAN PERÓN,
former Argentine dictator, who had been deposed in
1955, returns from exile to serve as president of Argentina, 1973. He died after ten months in office.

JAN SMUTS
resigns as prime minister of South Africa after the pro-
apartheid National party wins the parliamentary elections
of 1948.

FRANCISCO GOYA,
Spanish painter, leaves Spain and settles in Bordeaux,
France, where he does portraits, 1824.

MELVYN DOUGLAS
wins the 1979 Best Supporting Actor Academy Award for
Being There.

GENERAL KIM IL SUNG,
absolute dictator of North Korea, celebrates forty-five
years in office, 1990.

BERTRAND RUSSELL,
British mathematician, writer, and philosopher, wins the
1950 Nobel Prize for literature.

ANDRE GIDE
of France wins the 1947 Nobel Prize in literature.

ED WYNN,
veteran actor of vaudeville, radio, and television, appears
in the film *Mary Poppins*, 1964.

JOHN DEWEY,
American philosopher and educator, is part of an international commission that travels to investigate claims
against Leon Trotsky, 1937.

age seventy-nine

GLORIA SWANSON,
silent movie star, marries for the sixth time, 1976.

AYATOLLAH KHOMEINI
comes to power in Iran after the fall of the shah, 1979.

CHARLES DE GAULLE
resigns from the French presidency, 1969.

CLARA BARTON,
founder of the American Red Cross, organizes a national
relief effort after the Galveston Flood of 1900.

VICENTE ALEIXANDRE
of Spain wins the 1977 Nobel Prize in literature. This
was an important international moment of acceptance for
Spain, which was returning to democracy after the Franco
dictatorship ended in 1975.

GEORGES CLEMENCEAU
makes an unsuccessful bid for the French presidency,
1920.

age eighty

"Pick the right grandparents, don't eat or drink too much, be circumspect in all things, and take a two-mile walk before breakfast."
>—former President Harry S Truman, eighty, on his secret of a long life

"One does not leave a convivial party before closing time."
>—Sir Winston Churchill at eighty

"A human being would certainly not grow to be seventy or eighty years old if his longevity had no meaning for the species to which he belongs. The afternoon of human life must also have a significance of its own and cannot be merely a pitiful appendage to life's morning."
>Dr. Carl Gustav Jung, Swiss psychiatrist, who practiced into his eighties

*"The length of our days is seventy years—
or eighty, if we have the strength;
yet their span is but trouble and sorrow,
for they quickly pass and we fly away."*
>—Psalm 90:10

*"Pray, do not mock me.
I am a very foolish old man
Fourscore and upward; not an hour more or less
And to deal plainly
I fear I am not in my perfect mind."*
>—Shakespeare, *King Lear*

"Annus enim octogesimus admonet me ut sarcinas colligam, antequam proficiscare vita." *("For my eightieth year warns me to pack up my baggage before I leave life.")*

—Marcus Terentius Varro

GIUSEPPE VERDI,
Italian composer, composes his last opera, *Falstaff*, based on the character Sir John Falstaff from the Shakespeare play *The Merry Wives of Windsor*, 1893.

RALPH VAUGHAN WILLIAMS,
one of the greatest twentieth-century British composers, composes his *Sinfonia Antarctica*, 1952.

BORIS KARLOFF
appears in his last film, *The Incredible Invasion*, filmed in 1968 and released in 1971 after Karloff's death.

DR. SEUSS
wins a Special Citation Pulitzer Prize in honor of his contribution to American children's literature, 1984.

JESSICA TANDY
wins the 1989 Academy Award for *Driving Miss Daisy*.

GEORGE BURNS
wins the 1975 Best Supporting Actor Academy Award for *The Sunshine Boys*. He received the award, of course, in 1976, after his eightieth birthday.

LORD BERTRAND RUSSELL
marries for the fourth time, 1952.

FRANCISCO GOYA
resigns as court painter of Spain, 1826.

SAM JAFFE,
veteran character actor, appears in the Disney film *Bedknobs and Broomsticks*, 1971.

JOHN L. LEWIS
retires as president of the United Mine Workers of America, 1960.

JIMMY DURANTE
is still on the nightclub circuit, c. 1973.

GEORGES BRAQUE,
a cofounder of cubism with Picasso, is the first and only living artist to ever have his work displayed at the Louvre, Paris, 1962.

ALFRED P. SLOAN
retires as chairman of General Motors Corporation, 1956. When he became chairman in 1920, GM had a 12-percent share of the American automobile market. At the time of his retirement, GM held a 52-percent share.

age eighty-one

"When one has turned eighty-one, one likes to sit back and let the world turn by itself—without trying to push it."
—Irish playwright Sean O'Casey, *The New York Times*, September 25, 1960

BENJAMIN FRANKLIN
is elected delegate to the U.S. Constitutional Convention, 1787.

RALPH VAUGHAN WILLIAMS
composes music for the coronation of Queen Elizabeth II, 1953.

POPE JOHN XXIII
presides over the historic Second Vatican Council, a landmark in the modern Roman Catholic Church, 1962.

PABLO CASALS,
Spanish cellist, marries his pupil, Maria Montanez, sixty years his junior, 1957.

HENRI MATISSE,
French painter, thankful for the care given him by the Dominican Sisters at Vence, France, during an illness, creates a masterpiece—the Chapel of the Rosary at Vence, 1950–51.

JAMES CAGNEY,
after a twenty-year retirement from film, appears in his last film, *Ragtime*, 1981.

JOHANN WOLFGANG VON GOETHE,
greatest name in German literature, finishes writing
Faust, 1830.

RICHARD STRAUSS,
German composer, creates *Metamorfosen*, 1945.

age eighty-two

BERTRAND RUSSELL
writes *Human Society in Ethics and Politics*, 1954.

ALBERT SCHWEITZER
makes a public plea for international agreement to end
atomic weapons testing, 1957.

BENJAMIN FRANKLIN
is elected president of the first U.S. antislavery society,
1788.

SIGMUND FREUD
is driven from Vienna by the Nazis and settles in London, 1938.

ARTHUR FIEDLER
conducts the Boston Pops historic bicentennial concert of
July 4, 1976.

CONGRESSMAN CLAUDE PEPPER
leads the charge in Congress to defend social security
benefits, 1982.

LILLIAN GISH,
who had first appeared on film in 1912, appears in Robert
Altman's film *The Wedding*, appropriately as the grandmother, 1978.

GROUCHO MARX
is a hit on Broadway with his one-man show, *An Evening with Groucho*, 1972.

WINSTON CHURCHILL
writes *A History of the English-Speaking Peoples*, 1956.

COUNT LEO TOLSTOY
writes *I Cannot Be Silent*, 1910.

EAMON DE VALERA,
nearly eighty-three, is elected to a second term as president of the Republic of Ireland, 1966.

EDWARD STEICHEN,
pioneer American photographer, has his first one-man photographic exhibition at the New York Museum of Modern Art, 1961. Steichen said of photography: "Photography records the gamut of feelings on the human face, the beauty of the earth and skies that man has inherited, and the wealth and confusion man has created. It is a major force in explaining man to man. . . . We all cry and laugh but never at the same time or for the same reason. It's up to the photographer to catch the instant that is the reality of the person or of the moment" (*Time*, April 7, 1961).

PABLO PICASSO
is not slowed down by advancing age: his common-law wife, Françoise Gilot, the mother of their two children, leaves him after she learns he has been recently unfaithful, 1963.

age eighty-three

SIR WILLIAM EWART GLADSTONE
begins his last term as prime minister of Great Britain,
1892.

RUTH GORDON
appears in the film *Boardwalk*, 1979. She had first appeared in the film *Camille*, 1915, some sixty-four years
earlier.

NICHOLAS MURRAY BUTLER
retires as president of Columbia University, 1945.

NOAH WEBSTER
supervises the publication of a second edition of *An
American Dictionary of the English Language*, 1841.

ALEXANDER KERENSKY,
the interim prime minister of Russia before the Bolshevik
Revolution, writes *Russia and History's Turning Point*,
1964.

EAMON DE VALERA
is elected to another seven-year term as president of the
Republic of Ireland, 1966.

LEOPOLD STOKOWSKI
conducts the first complete performance of Charles Ives's
Fourth Symphony, 1965.

age eighty-four

"If you are small, death may quite likely overlook you."

—W. Somerset Maugham, eighty-four,
in *Time*, February 3, 1958

FRANZ JOSEF,
emperor of the Austro-Hungarian Empire, is this age at the beginning of World War I, 1914. Five years later, his empire would cease to exist.

MARSHAL HENRI PHILIPPE PETAIN
of France, a hero of World War I, becomes president of the Nazi puppet state of Vichy, France, 1940.

HERBERT HOOVER
former president of the United States, publishes his book *The Ordeal of Woodrow Wilson*, 1958.

JOHN MASEFIELD,
Poet Laureate of Great Britain, publishes his last collection of poems, 1961.

HENRI MATISSE,
French artist, is still experimenting with new forms, the "décollage" of paper cutouts to create *L'Escargot* ("The Snail"), 1953.

age eighty-five

"To me, old age is always fifteen years older than I am. . . . Age is only a number, a cipher for the records. A man can't retire his experience. He must use it. Experience achieves more with less energy and time."
—Bernard Baruch on his 85th birthday, 1955

SIR WILLIAM EWART GLADSTONE,
former prime minister of Great Britain, retires from Parliament, 1894.

MAE WEST
appears in the film *Sextette*, 1978.

CHARLES CHAPLIN
is knighted by Queen Elizabeth II, 1974.

TOMAS MASARYK,
father of the Czech republic, retires from the presidency, 1935.

EUBIE BLAKE,
pioneer ragtime pianist, makes a two-record album for Columbia Records, 1968.

CARL SANDBURG
publishes a new volume of poetry *Honey and Salt*, 1963.

age eighty-six

"As far as I can judge, with women it is all take and no give. There must be some women who are not liars. I do know a few women I am extremely fond of, but at my age one's attitude is rather different from a young man's."
— W. Somerset Maugham, eighty-six,
Time, October 17, 1960

CLARA BARTON,
founder of the American Red Cross, publishes her autobiography, 1907.

KONRAD ADENAUER
retires as chancellor of the German Federal Republic, 1963.

ROBERT FROST,
nearly eighty-seven, reads his poem "The Gift Outright" at the inauguration of President John F. Kennedy, 1961.

age eighty-seven

*"Most people say that as you get old, you have to
give things up. I say you get old because you give
things up."*
> —U.S. Senator Theodore Francis Green,
> on his eighty-seventh birthday

THEODORE FRANCIS GREEN,
Democrat of Rhode Island, quoted above, is elected to
another six-year term as a U.S. senator, 1954.

HERBERT HOOVER,
former president of the United States, finishes the third
and last volume of *An American Epic*, 1961.

ARTURO TOSCANINI
retires as conductor of the NBC Symphony, 1954.

JOHN WESLEY,
founder of Methodism, makes his last entry in his famous
journal, 1791.

BOB HOPE
travels to Saudi Arabia to entertain American troops in
Operation Desert Shield, 1990.

JOHN DEWEY,
American educator and philosopher, remarries and publishes *The Problems of Men*, 1947.

age eighty-eight

PABLO CASALS,
Spanish cellist, has a concert tour, 1964.

ARTHUR RUBINSTEIN,
Polish-born concert pianist, has a concert tour that in-
cludes a performance in Carnegie Hall, 1977–78.

LEOPOLD STOKOWSKI,
symphonic conductor, is busy making albums, 1970.

ARMAND HAMMER,
American industrialist, writes his autobiography, 1986.

MICHELANGELO
draws architectural plans for the Church of Santa Maria
Degli Angeli, 1553.

FRANK LLOYD WRIGHT,
American architect, begins work on the plans for the
Guggenheim Museum, New York, 1957. It was com-
pleted in 1959, when Wright was ninety.

age eighty-nine

"I am interested in physical medicine because my father was. I am interested in arthritis because I have it."
—Bernard M. Baruch, eighty-nine, 1959

MARSHAL HENRI PHILIPPE PETAIN
of France, head of the puppet Vichy government, is sentenced to death for collaboration with the Nazis, 1945. Through the intervention of Charles de Gaulle, the sentence was commuted to life imprisonment. Petain died in prison in 1951 at age ninety-five.

MARY BAKER EDDY
is at work every day at her office, directing the Church of Christ, Scientist, 1910.

ALBERT SCHWEITZER
is at work every day at his hospital in Gabon, West Africa, 1963.

old age

"More are men's ends mark'd than their lives before:
The setting sun, and music at the close,
As the last taste of sweets, is sweetest last
Writ in remembrance more than things long past."
— Shakespeare, *Richard III*

"No wise man ever wished to be younger."
— Jonathan Swift

"I shall grow old, but never lose life's zest.
Because the road's last turn will be the best."
— Henry Van Dyke

"And he died in a good old age, full of days, riches and honors."
I Chronicles 29:28

"What's a man's age?
He must hurry more, that's all;
Cram in a day what his youth took a year to hold."
— Robert Browning

"I confess that I am old; age is unnecessary."
— Shakespeare, *King Lear*

"To know how to grow old is the master-work of wisdom, and one of the most difficult chapters in the art of living."
— Henri Amiel

"It is only when you have lost your teeth that you can afford to eat steak!"

—Pierre Renoir, French painter

"All would live long, but none would be old."
—Ben Franklin, *Poor Richard's Almanac*

*"So mays't thou live till, like ripe fruit, thou drop
Into thy mother's lap, or be with ease
Gather'd, not harshly plucked, for death mature;
This is old age."*
—John Milton, *Paradise Lost*

*"The course of my long life hath reached at last,
In fragile bark oe'r a tempestuous sea
The common harbor, where must rendered be,
Account of all the actions of the past."*
—Henry Wadsworth Longfellow, "Old Age"

"[Age] has weathered the perilous capes and shoals in the sea whereon we sail, and the chief evil of life is taken away in removing the grounds of fear. . . . At every stage we lose a foe."

—Ralph Waldo Emerson

"With the ancient is wisdom, and with the length of days, understanding."

—Job, 12:12

"Most old people . . . are disheartened to be living in the ailing houses of their bodies, to be limited physically and economically, to feel an encumbrance to others—guests who didn't have the good manners to leave when the party was over."
—Barbara Walters, *How to Talk with Practically Anybody About Practically Anything*

"Youth is a blunder; manhood a struggle; old age a regret."
—Benjamin Disraeli, *Coningsby*

"The riders in a race do not stop when they reach the goal. There is still a little finishing canter before coming to a standstill. There is time to hear the kind voice of friends and to say to one's self—'The Work Is Done.' "

> —Justice Oliver Wendell Holmes, radio address
> on his ninetieth birthday, March 8, 1931

"Oh, what I wouldn't give to be seventy again!"

> —Justice Oliver Wendell Holmes, ninety-two,
> upon seeing an attractive woman

"You are only as old as the girls you feel."

> —George Burns, ninety, 1986

"Oh hell, another birthday . . ."

> —W. Somerset Maugham, on his ninety-first birthday, 1965

> *"Not till the fire is dying in the grate,*
> *Look we for any kinship with the stars."*
> > —George Meredith

"Certainly old age has a great sense of calm and freedom; when the passions relax their hold, then, as Sophocles says, you have escaped the control not of one master, but of many."

> —Plato, *The Republic*

> *"Whatever poet, orator or sage*
> *May say of it, old age is still old age.*
> *It is the waning, not the crescent moon;*
> *The dusk of evening, not the blaze of noon;*
> *It is not strength, but weakness; not desire,*
> *But its surcease; not the fierce heat of fire,*
> *The burning and consuming element,*
> *But that of ashes and of embers spent."*
> > —Henry Wadsworth Longfellow

*"Thus fares it still in our decay,
 And yet the wiser mind
 Mourns less for what age takes away
 Than what it leaves behind."*
 —Sir William Wordsworth

*"Thanks in old age—thanks ere I go
 For health, the midday sun, the impalpable air—
 for life, mere life
 For precious, ever lingering memory."*
 —Walt Whitman

"I agree that the last years of life are best if you are a philosopher."

George Santayana, American philosopher

*"To see a young couple loving each other is a wonder; but to
see an old couple loving each other is the best sight of all."*
 —William Makepeace Thackeray

*"My candle burns at both ends
 It will not last the light
 But ah, my friends, and oh, my foes
 It gives a lovely light."*
 —Edna St. Vincent Millay

*"Growing old is no more than a bad habit which a busy man
has no time to form."*

—Andre Maurois

*"Life is precious to the old person. He is not interested merely
in the thoughts of yesterday's good life and tomorrow's path to
the grave. He does not want his later years to be a sentence of
solitary confinement in society. Nor does he want them to be a
death watch."*
 —Dr. David Allman, American gerontologist, 1959

"Life is something like this trumpet. If you don't put anything in it, you don't get anything out. And that's the truth."
—W. C. HANDY, the "Father of the Blues,"
eighty-five, 1958

"Old age is not for sissies."

—Katharine Hepburn

some famous people who lived into their ninetieth year

(NOTE: Most of these have entries elsewhere in the *Book of Ages*.)

JOHN ADAMS, 1735–1826
second president of the United States. He and Thomas Jefferson both died on the fiftieth anniversary of American Independence, July 4, 1826.

KONRAD ADENAUER, 1876–1967
First Chancellor of the German Federal Republic, he retired in 1963 at age eighty-seven.

BERNARD M. BARUCH, 1870–1965
American financier and statesman. Baruch was a young wonder on Wall Street during the 1890s and 1900s, and was a millionaire by age forty. He organized the supply of raw materials for the American war effort during World War I and served as an adviser to virtually every American president from Wilson to Kennedy.

GEORGE BURNS, born January 20, 1896
American actor who won an Oscar at age eighty and is still performing. He has booked the London Palladium for his one hundredth birthday in 1996.

PABLO CASALS, 1876–1973
Spanish concert cellist who was still giving recitals at age ninety.

MARC CHAGALL, 1887–1985
Russian-born, French artist.

GIORGIO DI CHIRICO, 1887–1978
influential Italian psychological painter who later abandoned the avant garde in favor of more traditional forms.

SIR WINSTON S. CHURCHILL, 1874–1965
served as prime minister of Great Britain, 1940–45, and again from 1951 to 1955. He retired from Parliament at age ninety in 1964.

MARC CONNELLY, 1890–1980
American playwright, won a Pulitzer Prize in 1930 for *Green Pastures*, based on black spirituals.

PETER COOPER, 1791–1883
built the first commercial railroad in North America.

AARON COPLAND, 1900–1990
American composer.

EAMON DE VALERA, 1882–1975
served as president of Ireland and was reelected at age eighty-three, retiring from the presidency at ninety-one.

WILLIAM DEMAREST, 1892–1982
American character actor who played Uncle Charlie on the 1960s television series "My Three Sons."

JOHN DEWEY, 1859–1952
American philosopher and educator, advocate of "radical empiricism." Published books into his nineties.

DAVID DUBINSKY, 1892–1982
American labor leader born in Russian Poland. He was exiled to Siberia for labor activity in Russian Poland and was a leader of both the International Ladies' Garment

Workers Union (vice-president) and the AFL-CIO (vice-president).

HARRY EMERSON FOSDICK, 1878–1968
one of America's most influential Protestant churchmen and pastor of the Riverside Church, New York. Fosdick was an advocate of reconciling science and religion in opposition to religious fundamentalism.

JOHN VANCE GARNER, 1868–1967
vice-president of the United States, 1933–41. "Cactus Jack," as he was known, opposed President Roosevelt's decision to seek a third term and is remembered for his quote "Being vice-president isn't worth a bucket of warm spit."

HERMIONE GINGOLD, 1897–1987
veteran British character actress and delightful talk-show guest.

SAMUEL GOLDWYN, 1882–1974
one of the most important American film producers of all time.

ROBERT GRAVES, 1895–1985
British classical scholar and author. He wrote the two successful novels of ancient Rome, *I, Claudius* and *Claudius the God*. He also wrote *The White Goddess*, an important study of mythology.

HELEN HAYES, born October 10, 1900
one of the greatest American actresses of stage and screen of the twentieth century. Miss Hayes is still active in 1991 as a spokesperson for the U.S. space program.

KNUT HAMSUN, 1859–1952
Norwegian novelist who won the 1920 Nobel Prize in literature.

W. AVERELL HARRIMAN, 1891–1986
American diplomat, governor of New York, and negotiator of the Nuclear Test Ban Treaty of 1963.

STANLEY HOLLOWAY, 1890–1982
British actor noted for his role as the father of Eliza Doolittle in the 1964 film *My Fair Lady*.

JUSTICE OLIVER WENDELL HOLMES, JR., 1841–1935
an associate justice of the Supreme Court, writer, philosopher, and scholar.

JULIA WARD HOWE, 1819–1910
one of the most famous women writers and lecturers of her day. She composed "The Battle Hymn of the Republic."

OSKAR KOKOSCHKA, 1886–1980
Austrian-born painter who became a British subject in 1947. He was famous for his "psychological" portraits and steadfastly held to the pre–World War I expressionist style of painting.

ALFRED A. KNOPF, 1892–1984
founder of the publishing firm of the same name.

S. S. KRESGE, 1867–1966
founder of the Kresge and K mart merchandising chains.

ALICE ROOSEVELT LONGWORTH, 1884–1980
Daughter of President Theodore Roosevelt, she scandalized the public by smoking in public during her father's presidency. Later, she married Nicholas Longworth, Speaker of the U.S. House of Representatives, and was an important Washington socialite and wit.

ARCHIBALD MACLEISH, 1892–1982
American diplomat, poet, and author. He won the 1933

Pulitzer Prize in Poetry for *Conquistador*, an epic recounting of Cortés's invasion of Mexico. In 1955, he won another Pulitzer Prize, this time in drama, for the play *J.B.*

JOAN MIRO, 1893–1983
Spanish painter.

VYACHESLAV MOLOTOV, 1890–1986
former Soviet Foreign Minister during the 1940s and 1950s. The "molotov cocktail," a bomb consisting of a jar of gasoline with a rag in it, is named for him.

ROBERT MOSES, 1888–1981
One of the most important men in the development of modern New York City, he served as commissioner of parks and as president of the 1964 World's Fair.

FLORENCE NIGHTINGALE, 1820–1910
One of the best-known British women of her day, she set up the battlefield hospitals during the Crimean War. Known as the "Lady With the Lamp," she remains a pivotal figure in the history of nursing.

GEORGIA O'KEEFE, 1887–1986
celebrated American painter and wife of photographer Alfred Stieglitz.

HERBERT HOOVER, 1874–1964
president of the United States from 1929 to 1933; published his last historical works at age eighty-seven.

LEVI P. MORTON, 1824–1920
vice-president of the United States under President Benjamin Harrison, 1889–93.

LORD BERTRAND RUSSELL, 1872–1970
British mathematician, philosopher, pacifist, and writer.

J. C. PENNEY, 1875-1971
founder of the department-store chain. Started from scratch with one general store in Wyoming and retired with over 1,900 stores.

WILLIAM POWELL, 1892–1984
American actor best known for his portrayal of Nick Charles in *The Thin Man* series of films.

PABLO PICASSO, 1881–1973
Spanish painter who remained artistically, and sexually, active into his nineties.

ISIDOR ISAAC RABI, 1898–1988
American physicist who won the 1944 Nobel Prize in physics.

A. PHILIP RANDOLPH, 1889–1979
One of the greatest leaders in the African-American civil rights movement, he organized the Pullman Porters' strike of the 1920s and remained a powerful civil rights advocate through the 1960s.

JOHN D. ROCKEFELLER, 1837–1939
founder of Standard Oil and one of the richest men in history.

ARTHUR RUBINSTEIN, 1887–1982
great Polish-American concert pianist. As a young man, he once considered suicide, but afterward devoted himself to living life to the fullest. He continued to give piano concerts into his nineties.

ALBERT SCHWEITZER, 1875–1965
Alsatian theologian, organist, and medical missionary.

ANDRES SEGOVIA, 1893–1987
Spanish classical guitarist, recorded into his nineties.

JAN SIBELIUS, 1865–1957
Finland's greatest composer.

UPTON SINCLAIR, 1878–1968
American journalist and author.

ALFRED P. SLOAN, 1875–1965
American business leader and philanthropist. Was president of General Motors Corporation from 1920 to 1956. Benefactor of the Sloan Museum and the Sloan-Kettering Cancer Institute.

LEOPOLD STOKOWSKI, 1882–1977
British-American conductor, was working on a new recording when he died at age ninety-five.

ARTURO TOSCANINI, 1867–1957
Italian-American conductor.

LOUIS UNTERMEYER, 1885–1977
American editor and anthologist.

DEWITT WALLACE, 1889–1981
founder of *Reader's Digest*.

REVEREND NORMAN VINCENT PEALE, born 1898
publishes *The Power of Positive Living*, 1990.

VITTORIO EMMANUELE ORLANDO, 1860–1952
prime minister of Italy and one of the big four at the Versailles Peace Conference of 1919.

DAME REBECCA WEST, 1892–1983
British novelist and companion of H. G. Wells.

GLUYAS WILLIAMS, 1888–1982
American cartoonist who illustrated Robert Benchley's books and frequently contributed to the *New Yorker* magazine.

P. G. WODEHOUSE 1881–1975
British-American author and satirist, creator of Jeeves and Bertie Wooster.

SIR CHRISTOPHER WREN, 1632–1723
British architect who designed St. Paul's Cathedral, London.

FRANK LLOYD WRIGHT, 1869–1959
America's greatest architect.

EFREM ZIMBALIST, SR., 1889–1985
Russian-born concert violinist, father of actor Efrem Zimbalist, Jr., and grandfather of actress Stephanie Zimbalist.

the nineties

age ninety

FRANK LLOYD WRIGHT,
American architect, completes the design of the Guggenheim Museum, New York, 1959.

JOHN DEWEY,
American educator and philosopher, publishes *Knowing and the Known*, 1949.

JEANNETTE RANKIN,
former congresswoman from Montana, leads an anti–Vietnam War march, 1972.

SIR WINSTON S. CHURCHILL
retires from Parliament, 1964.

age ninety-one

EAMON DE VALERA
retires as president of the Republic of Ireland, 1973.

ADOLPH ZUKOR
is chairman of the board of Paramount Pictures, 1964.

age ninety-two

REVEREND NORMAN VINCENT PEALE, born 1898
author of *The Power of Positive Thinking*, 1952, who
published *The Power of Positive Living* in 1990 at age
ninety-two.

age ninety-three

GEORGE BERNARD SHAW
writes *Farfetched Fables*, 1949.

W.E.B. DUBOIS,
African-American writer and activist, known for his ear-
lier work *The Souls of Black Folk*, joins the American
Communist party, 1961.

age ninety-four

LORD BERTRAND RUSSELL
organizes an international disarmament drive, 1966.

EUBIE BLAKE,
pioneer ragtime piano artist, performs on television and
at the White House, 1977.

W.E.B. DUBOIS
renounces his American citizenship and becomes a citizen of Ghana, 1962.

age ninety-five

LEOPOLD STOKOWSKI
is hard at work on his last recording, 1977.

age ninety-six

BARBARA FRIETCHIE,
according to the poem by John Greenleaf Whittier, refuses to lower the U.S. flag as Confederate troops march into Frederick, Maryland, 1862. " 'Shoot, if you must, this old gray head, but spare your country's flag,' she said." To which the Confederate commander replied, " 'Whoever touches a hair on your gray head, dies like a dog. March on!' "

age one hundred plus

EUBIE BLAKE, 1883–1983
American ragtime pianist.

ADOLPH ZUKOR, 1873–1976
chairman of the Board of Paramount Pictures until age ninety-one.

WALTER WILLIAMS, 1842–1959
A Confederate veteran, Mr. Williams of Houston, Texas, was the last surviving veteran of the Civil War. He died on August 2, 1959, at age 117.

ALBERT WOOLSON, 1847–1956
The last surviving Union veteran of the Civil War, Mr. Woolson of Duluth, Minnesota, died on August 2, 1956, at age 109.

GEORGE ABBOTT, born June 25, 1887
American playwright, film director and producer, alive at the time of this writing in 1991. Mr. Abbott is best known for his musicals *Damn Yankees* and *The Pajama Game*.

SHIRALI MISLIMOV, 1805–1973
A resident of Azerbaijan, USSR, Mislimov claimed to be 168 years old; however, this could not be documented. (Source: *The People's Almanac 2* by David Wallechinsky and Irving Wallace, Bantam Books, 1978.)

CHARLIE SMITH, 1842–1978
A former slave, Smith claimed to have been brought to the United States from Africa. His age could not be documented. He allegedly worked in the fields until age 113. (Source: Ibid.)

SHIGECHIYO IZUMI, 1865–1986
According to *The Guinness Book of World Records*, Mr. Izumi is the oldest authenticated living person. He died at age 120 years, 237 days, on February 21, 1986.

LIAKOUS EFDOKIA, 1864–1982
of Greece. The oldest authenticated age attained by a female. (Source: *Guinness Book of World Records*.)

PIERRE JOUBERT, 1701–1814
the oldest authenticated age of any Canadian. (Source: *Guinness Book of World Records*.)

KATHERINE PLUNKETT, 1820–1932
the oldest authenticated age of a British subject. (Sources: *Guinness Book of World Records* and *The People's Almanac 2*.)

the super old of the bible

ADAM,
the first man, 930 years.

SETH,
son of Adam, 912 years.

ENOCH,
who was taken into heaven by God, 365 years.

METHUSELAH,
the oldest person in the Bible, 969 years. He is said to
have died the year of the Great Flood.

NOAH,
captain of the ark, 950 years.

ABRAHAM,
patriarch of ancient Israel, was one hundred when his
son Isaac was born, and his wife Sarah was ninety. Sarah
died at age 127, and Abraham, according to the book of
Genesis, lived to be 175.

MOSES,
according to the Bible, died at 120.

the last chapter

"We have passed Age's icy caves,
And Manhood's dark and tossing waves
And Youth's smooth ocean, smiling to betray:
Beyond the glassy gulfs we flee
of shadow-peopled infancy
Through Death and Birth to a diviner day."
                    —Shelley, *Prometheus Unbound*

"The great world of light lies
Beyond all human destinies."
—Henry Wadsworth Longfellow

"This life is but the passage of a day,
This life is but a pang and all is over
But in the life to come which fades not away
Every love shall abide and every lover."
  —Christina Rossetti, "Saints and Angels"

"Sunset and evening star
And one clear call for me!
And may there be no moaning of the bar
When I put out to sea
For tho' from out our bourne of time and place
The flood may bear me far
I hope to see my Pilot face to face
When I have crost the bar."
   —Alfred, Lord Tennyson, "Crossing the Bar"

"Think not disdainfully of death, but look on it with favor, for Nature wills it like all else . . . look for the hour when the soul shall emerge from its sheath, as now you await the moment when the child emerges from your wife's womb."

—Marcus Aurelius, *Meditations*

> *"Joy, shipmate, joy*
> *(Pleas'd to my soul at death I cry)*
> *Our life is closed, our life begins,*
> *The long, long anchorage we leave*
> *The ship is clear at last, she leaps!*
> *She quickly courses from the shore*
> *Joy, shipmate, joy."*

—Walt Whitman

"If there is a Universal and Supreme Consciousness, I am an idea in it; and it is possible for any idea in this Supreme Consciousness to be completely blotted out? After I have died, God will go on remembering me, and to be remembered by God, to have my consciousness sustained by the Supreme Consciousness, is not that, perhaps, to live?"

—Miguel de Unamuno, *The Tragic Sense of Life*

> *"Fool! All that is, at all*
> *Lasts ever past recall;*
> *Earth changes, but thy soul and God stand sure:*
> *What entered into thee*
> *That was, is, and shall be:*
> *Time's wheel runs back or stops;*
> *Potter and clay endure."*

—Robert Browning, "Rabbi Ben Ezra"

"As the mother's womb holds us for ten months, making us ready, not for the womb itself, but for life, just so, through our lives, we are making ourselves ready for another birth. . . . Therefore look forward without fear to that appointed hour—the last hour of the body, but not of the soul. . . . That day, which you fear as being the end of all things, is the birthday of your eternity."

—Seneca

"No, no, I'm sure,
My restless spirit never could endure
To brood so long upon one luxury,
Unless it did, though fearfully espy
A hope beyond the shadow of a dream."

John Keats, *Endymion*

"For I know that my Redeemer lives, and at last He shall stand upon the earth; and after my skin is thus destroyed, then without flesh I shall see God, whom I shall see at my side."

—Job, 19:21–27

"For God so loved the world that he gave his only son, that whoever believes in Him should not perish, but have eternal life."

—John, 3:16

About the Author

At the time of *The Book of Ages*'s completion, J. F. Bierlein reached the age of thirty-five, which meant:

- —he was now old enough to run for president but declined to accept the nomination;
- —he was too old to join the FBI; but
- —he had outlived a lot of famous people.

From 1979 to 1983, J. F. Bierlein was the librarian at the Democratic National Committee in Washington, D.C., and later a congressional aide; and was an active participant in the 1980 Democratic National Convention. *The Book of Ages* is a product of his years in Washington as a researcher and speechwriter. Mr. Bierlein, a religion teacher, is active in jail ministry and counseling, and in issues affecting the developmentally disabled and mentally ill. Multilingual, he is an ardent environmentalist whose eclectic interests include the study of classical Greek and Hebrew, philosophy, archaeology, Latin American art, opera, and antiques. He has just completed a novel, *Canadian Missed*, and a study of myth, *The Eternal Mirror*. He lives in Frankenmuth, Michigan, where he is currently at work on a new novel and a study of existentialism.